GURU

Born in Bangalore in 1954, poet and playwright H.S. Shivaprakash is considered one of the most influential voices in Kannada literature. A recipient of the Sahitya Akademi Award and the Sangeet NatakAkademi Award, he has also received the highest awards in Karnataka for literature and drama. His literary works have been translated into most Indian languages, as well as into English, Spanish, German, French and Italian. A scholar on the Indian bhakti traditions, he is also the author of *Everyday Yogi and I Keep Vigil of Rudra*. Professor Shivaprakash teaches theatre studies at the School of Arts and Aesthetics, Jawaharlal Nehru University, New Delhi. He is also Honorary Fellow at the School of Letters, University of Iowa, USA.

GURU

TEN DOORS TO ANCIENT WISDOM

H.S. SHIVAPRAKASH

First published in 2018 by Hachette India
(Registered name: Hachette Book Publishing India Pvt. Ltd)
An Hachette UK company
www.hachetteindia.com

This edition published in 2021

SRD

ISBN 978-93-5195-243-5

Hachette Book Publishing India Pvt. Ltd
4th/5th Floors, Corporate Centre,
Plot No. 94, Sector 44, Gurugram 122003, India

Typeset in Minion Pro 11/15.7
by InoSoft Systems Noida

Printed and bound in India
by Manipal Technologies Limited, Manipal

MIX
Paper from
responsible sources
FSC
www.fsc.org FSC™ C104740

To my mother, who was the first guru
And to my guru, the mother of mothers

Hamsabhyam parivrittam
Harde kamale shuddhe
Jagatkaranam vishwakaram
Anekadehanilayam
Swachchandamanandakam
Sarvadharam akhanda chidanndaghnarasam
Poornamhyanantam shubham
Pratyakshaksharavigraham guruvaram
Dhyayed vibhum shaswatam.

Surrounded by swans
In the purity of the heart-lotus
He is the cause of the whole universe
And the dweller in countless bodies
Still free of all and full of bliss
He is the basis of all
And the absolute bliss of consciousness
Perfect, eternal and auspicious
Let me meditate on the Guru
The visible embodiment of the World
The Lord who is eternal.

Contents

Contents

BEFORE APPROACHING THE DOORS...

THIS BOOK INTRODUCES AND EXAMINES CONCEPTS THAT are essential to Indian spiritual traditions, with a view to help you enter the fascinating world of spiritual practice. You will be taken to the threshold of ten important spiritual doors, and given a glimpse of what lies within. Then, if there is a desire to enter, you are free to do so according to your taste and temperament. Entering a chamber presents the opportunity to explore, experiment with and experience the spiritual wisdom and truths that are contained therein.

Though the concepts and metaphors that make up the bricks and mortar of this book are taken from different streams of ancient Indian spiritual traditions, the book does not follow in entirety a specific school like Buddhism, Jainism or Vedanta. Nor is it a full-fledged philosophical exploration of any particular school.

Further, while not an advertisement or a critique of any sect or cult, this book contests sweeping claims made by sects, cults and religions, without losing sight of the essential unity of spiritual experiences they seek to explicate. I would also like to make clear that this book does not intend to be a manual of specific spiritual practices like asanas, pranayama or meditation.

This book is an amalgamation of Indian spiritual and philosophical theory, and my personal experiences. While I have leaned on the major Indian schools of thought for their key concepts and ideas, I have presented them to you through the lens of my own personal spiritual experiments and experiences.

Hardened doubters or blind followers do not need this book; neither do people already enlightened. It is for those in between, seekers and sceptics who are unable to believe easily and insist on experiential validation. While not promising to answer all the questions that may occur to you on the subject of Indian spirituality, this book is intended to enrich your life by connecting you with ideas, practices and experiences that can lead to positive transformation, provided you are willing to explore them. Come to this book with an open mind, and it may give you something you have been looking for.

When my publisher suggested that I write a book on ten fundamentally 'Indic' spiritual concepts, it took me quite some time to zero in on the essential ones. Though the ultimate goal of the spiritual journey is the end of suffering and the attainment of joy and freedom, every traveller on this path experiences its joys and sorrows differently, as each person is unique. As Sri Ramakrishna said: 'Joto mota, totho patho' (there are as many paths as there are temperaments).

Further, the nature of spiritual experience is completely subjective even though, after inner transformation, its effects become visible on the intersubjective plane. What one has experienced and realized subjectively can be communicated and transmitted to others so that they can experience and realize things subjectively at their own level of understanding.

Hence, the main challenge I faced was to identify a finite set of concepts that could hold across widely different personality types. And since spirituality is ultimately about experience, the concepts had to have a practical validity. Each concept, I felt, must be like a door that opens to a rich world of subjective experiences. It is at this point that I began to feel that the metaphor of the door can take us closer to the experiential dimension of spirituality. Metaphors have always seemed to me to be more concrete than concepts.

Once the metaphor of the door was established in my mind, I had to give a name to each one of the ten doors. I see the word 'guru' inscribed on the main door.

A guru is a spiritual teacher who has the knowledge and experience to initiate and guide the seeker through his spiritual journey. Depending on the nature of the guru and the system he follows, the guru then takes the practitioner to other chambers. For instance, if the guru happens to be a mantra guru, he can lead one to the mantra chamber.

For some people, the mantra door is the first to open, and eventually leads them to the guru and/or the devata, the deity. It is the mantra that binds the guru and the seeker together. All mantras carry divine energy, but it is divine energy that is actually the devata. I give this example of the guru, mantra and devata to show you that, in the world of spiritual practice, these chambers are interconnected, and one chamber can open to other chambers.

Thus, there is flexibility in entering these doors. You do not necessarily have to start your journey with a guru or a mantra. You could be someone who is more comfortable connecting with a deity, so you can start your journey there. The deity can later connect you to mantra practice and to the guru, and then to other rooms.

There are certain people who, given their temperaments, need to go through some of the doors but not all of them. Such people may find fulfillment in one of these chambers as they move along, and therefore do not need to explore further chambers.

Interestingly, it is equally possible that the seeker finds everything he needs in one particular chamber – the very first chamber he enters. For the steadfast, just one door is enough. If one's focus is absolute, one can see the ocean in a mere drop. For instance, someone may connect with a guru, or a deity, and is able to reach the Divine just through that path.

These days, the body is the easiest door to enter for most people, as they live on the physical plane. By this, I mean that people are deeply influenced by the materialism of the modern world. Yet, being attached to the body does not have to be an obstacle on the spiritual path. In fact, some of our spiritual traditions like yoga and tantra have considered the body to be a temple of the Divine. It is not necessary to bruise the body to pleasure the soul; the body can be a means to reach the soul.

Different body techniques, postures and movements lead to the realization that the body consists of subtle psychic energies. When a person achieves a certain degree of ease with asanas, he will start feeling subtler energies flowing in the body. Focusing on the body can, sooner or later, usher one to others chambers like the breath and the mind. But, as I have explained, the body can also be the end in itself.

Now, there are people whose awareness is focused more on the breath than the body, and they are able to enter the spiritual realm through the breath. Breath is the elusive bond between body and mind. It is 'elusive' because most people know how the body or the mind feels but not how the breath feels. A whole range of breath practices, such as pranayama and pranavidya, has been evolved to help them.

One can also enter the spiritual plane through the mind. In raja yoga, which is the yoga of the mind, the significance of physical training is minimal; all one needs for mental practice is a stable and relaxed sitting posture and some degree of breath control to enable the mind to settle on the object of concentration.

Sometimes, you will encounter difficulties or blocks in your sadhana, and this may necessitate experiencing other rooms so that those blocks are cleared. For example, you can be someone who is enthusiastic enough to go straight to meditation, but discover that pain in some part of the body is absorbing all your attention. It may then be necessary to go through the physical practice of hatha yoga before resuming meditation.

There are some people who, possessing the subtlest of sensibilities, can walk directly into the chamber of anuttara. This is the final stage of spiritual practice, and it is only a highly evolved being who can reach here directly.

Some schools of spirituality hold stillness to be the goal of spiritual evolution. Ascetic schools of spirituality enjoin a withdrawal from all action into silence and stillness. Their view is that engagement with the world will result in blindness to the light within. But, as I have explained earlier, this approach of the denial of the world will not suit most people as they want to be a part of the material world.

Having said this, it is perfectly possible to meet the Divine by being active in the world. The very purpose of this book is to show you how you can have a spiritual practice and be able to attain the Supreme by being here and now. All the concepts I have presented in this book are ways of living a spiritual life as an ordinary person. Spiritual freedom is to be found *in* the world of actions, not away from it.

Kama (desire and sexuality); karma and kayaka (action and labour); and pratibha (creative energy), are three other doors you will encounter, and they are also interconnected. These three chambers are related to creativity, and constitute the primal urge to participate in creation through procreation, work and creative expressions.

The last door that this book takes you to is anuttara, unsurpassed experience. It exists even beyond the states of moksha, nirvana or kevala jnana. Like all parts of the tree becoming the tree, like all drops in the ocean becoming the ocean, all other doors become dimensions of anuttara – the principle of eternity, hidden in the fluctuations of space–time. The most blessed of seekers, who are few and far between, can directly enter and 'become' this state.

To better understand the interconnectedness of the doors, visualize them not in the plain two-dimensional space of Euclidean geometry but in the transformational space of non-Euclidean geometry, where spaces curve away and into each other. We can enter the inner realm from any one of the ten doors, for these doors collapse into one another, lead to each other and become each other in the constantly pulsating and multi-dimensional space of anuttara. I request you to keep these points in mind while reading this book.

I would like to mention that all the English translations, unless mentioned otherwise, are my own. Go ahead and start reading, opening any one of the ten doors, for all of them lead to anuttara – your own essential self, synonymous with light and freedom.

Door 1

GURU

THE GURU IS USUALLY THE FIRST DOOR A SEEKER
opens as he sets out on his spiritual journey because
relating to, and being guided by, a master is often the
easiest way to embark on the spiritual path. Lord Shiva
says in the *Shiva Sutras*, 'Gururupaayam', the guru is
the means.

The guru, in simple terms, is a teacher, but he is
unlike other teachers. Ordinary teachers impart to
us knowledge about different subjects in the material
world; a guru is a spiritual teacher who lights up the
path *within*. The skills and knowledge that he bestows
upon us belong to the inner world. Like the mythical
philosopher's stone, which converts base metal into
gold, a guru's teachings transform the limited and
conditioned self into unlimited and unconditioned
awareness. The guru has the ability to bring about

complete inner transformation, taking the disciple from the darkness of ignorance to the light of wisdom, from suffering to joy. Basavanna, a twelfth-century poet and philosopher, says:

> *Madakeya maduvare manne modalu*
> *Todigeya maaduvare hone modalu*
> *Shivapthavanarivare gurupathave modalu*
> *Kudalasangamadev.*

> (If you want to make a pot
> Start with the earth,
> If you want to make an ornament
> Start with gold,
> If you want to understand Shiva's path
> Start with the guru's path,
> O Lord Kudalasangama.)

The spiritual journey is a dynamic one. Though the goal remains constant, the nature of the journey is always changing. Spiritual evolution is neither a linear nor a step-by-step process; nor does it develop on the lines of an existing formula. Instead, it is a road full of ups and downs, twists and turns, advances and retreats, unexpected blockages and equally unpredictable breakthroughs. It is, in short, full of surprises, and not all of them are pleasant.

The needs of seekers differ depending on where they have reached in their quest for inner freedom. When a person starts her journey with a guru, she needs to be able to relate to a human being. This is the stage of dependence that is necessary for most of us to start with because we exist in a dualistic consciousness.

It is only much later, when the seeker has advanced along the spiritual path, does she realize that the guru is actually *within*. So, whether the guru is experienced within or without depends on the level of the disciple's consciousness. The external guru is a manifestation of the inner guru, the principle of limitless joy and freedom within us.

The biggest hurdle in spiritual practice is the ego. The surrender to a physical guru gradually results in the dissolution of the ego. Here, I hasten to point out the vital difference between a genuine guru and a charlatan. A true master is connected to the Divine and only seeks the disciple's growth. True gurus are endowed with great spiritual energy, and are able to transfer this energy to the disciple.

The greater the spiritual energy the guru shares with the disciple, the closer they get. Then, there is a stage in the disciple's spiritual evolution where the dependence is transformed into a union with the guru who, by then, has been internalized in the being of the disciple. This is when a true disciple and guru merge into each other.

And when the drop merges with the ocean, the ocean also merges with the drop. When the guru becomes part of us, he is not a person anymore but a principle. When the guru ceases to be an individual, so does the disciple. Allama Prabhu, one of the greatest spiritual poets of Karnataka, wrote in the twelfth century:

Guruve shishyanaada tanna vinodakke
Shishyane guruvada tanna vinodakke.

(The guru became the disciple for his fun
And the disciple became the guru for his fun.)

Though the guru's energy is very powerful, it works even better when the disciple's heart is open to the guru in unconditional surrender. According to Purandara Dasa, a sixteenth-century saint-singer of Karnataka:

Guruvina gulamanaguva tanaka
Doreyadanna mukuti.

(Unless you become the guru's slave
You will not get salvation, brother.)

A true guru always leads us beyond the I-and-you stage. When he takes us to the highest stage of intuitive knowledge, there is neither 'I' nor 'you' but only 'It': the light and joy within and without. The ultimate purpose of the guru–disciple relationship is unconditional freedom and the end of all kinds of dependence, including the dependence on the guru.

The inability to understand this leads to a lot of confusion and frustrations on the spiritual path. Militant followers of gurus start worshipping the human receptacle, not realizing that the guru is only the means to the divine essence within *them*. Disciples become so dependent on the person identified as the guru that they, like blinkered horses, cannot get beyond him. The result is that they lose themselves instead of finding their inner truth, which is the very purpose of the guru's role in their growth.

Gurus aren't free of the pitfalls of the ego either. Many a guru has succumbed to the adoration of his disciples and the power that has come his way as a result, and has become a spiritual tyrant instead of a wise master, demanding *he* be worshipped. There are, of course, many charlatans about the place as well, who manage to fool countless people into believing that they are beings full of spiritual power, when they are just glib talkers who prey on the vulnerabilities and gullibility of people looking for help and guidance. These people want their disciples to depend on them completely, for that is how their need for power is satisfied.

Occasionally, a disciple will discover this 'guru' for what he truly is, but is too afraid to leave, fearing his wrath. Such a guru–disciple relationship is unwholesome and false as it is based on fear and manipulation, and not on any genuine spiritual evolution or truth.

———

The guru enters into a deep relationship with the disciple through the process of initiation. The methods of initiation vary according to the nature of the training the guru imparts to the disciple; this, in turn, depends on the disciple's character, requirements and stage of evolution. Initiation can take place in different ways, for example, with a mantra, through meditation or even physical touch.

Though the goal of all spiritual practices is the attainment of inner freedom, there are different paths to attain this goal. Disciples whose identification with the physical plane is strong find external rituals or physical methods like hatha yoga easier to respond to. Others find it easier to take to breath or mind-based practices like pranayama, mantra or meditation. Whichever method the guru uses to initiate the disciple, the intitation happens due to the shaktipat, energy transmission, from the guru to the disciple.

There are some exceptional disciples who are already extremely evolved, and their spiritual nature just needs to be awakened. A guru can do this with energy transmission through touch or a mere glance. Sri Ramakrishna initiated Vivekananda just by his touch. Ramana Maharshi did not even need a human guru because he received shaktipat directly from Lord Shiva.

Not all gurus are at the same level of evolution, and neither are disciples. The nature of a disciple and his stage of evolution usually determine the kind of guru he will attract. Therefore, a guru can be human or even divine depending on the caliber of the disciple.

This can be illustrated with the story of Milarepa, a renowned Tibetan yogi. When he was young, his family suffered greatly at the hands of his aunt and uncle. His mother asked him to study black magic so they could take revenge. With single-minded dedication, he mastered the black art for several years and then attacked his aunt and uncle. However, when his black magic guru fell fatally ill at some point, he wondered why his master was not using his magical powers to heal himself. The guru then explained that his powers could only destroy people; they could not be used for any positive purpose. He advised Milarepa not to waste his life doing black magic but to seek a master who could truly liberate him.

Milarepa then went to a spiritual master called Lotsawa Marpa, who put him through countless ordeals to purify him from the bad karmas accumulated through his use of black magic. It was only then that Milarepa evolved into an exemplary yogi. After years of austerities, he attained oneness with Marpa and became a guru himself.

Allama Prabhu describes the experience of the guru–disciple relationship thus:

Tell me
Before I became aware of myself, what were you?
You had shut your mouth up
I saw it through your eyes
Now that I have become aware of myself
If you open your mouth and speak
I see it through your eyes
And feel shy
For me seeing you and you seeing me
The relationship is the same
Look, O Goggeshwara
I have figured out the mystery of this paradox.

Many disciples stick to their gurus as long as they see their own idea of the guru in him. But a true guru is interested in the disciple's growth and not in perpetuating the disciple's limited idea of him. For example, a disciple may be looking for a guru to whom he can hand over the responsibility for his life and choices, while the guru seeks to liberate the disciple from that very dependency. Here, a disciple may fear the hard lesson he is being taught, and seek to escape this guru. Still, a true guru's intent is always the disciple's spiritual growth.

Where can we find the right guru? Even if we find one, can we recognize him? The answer to this is that if and when the disciple is ready, the guru comes to him.

It is also possible that the same person may find different gurus at different phases of his life. I, for example, have had not one but several gurus. Sri Ramakrishna had three gurus, and so did Yogi Ramsuratkumar.

Each time I found a guru, it felt to me like I had found my ideal guru. For a considerable period of time, I would stay loyal to him. But, one day, suddenly, the bond would snap, leaving a great void in me. I would soon find another guru but only to repeat the same painful pattern of events. I discovered I could not stay with a single guru, and I was very disturbed by this because I felt I was being disloyal. I held the belief that the guru–chela relationship was as indissoluble as the bond involved in monogamy.

Finally, I came to realize that the Guru is a principle and not a person, and that all physical gurus are the limited manifestations of the Cosmic Guru. Then, I was able to let go of my guilt and anguish. I was also able to understand that my gurus came to me when I needed them for my growth, and they left when my work with them was over.

Just as light can be glimpsed only in the light of light, the guru can be found with the light of the Cosmic Guru. All physical or human gurus are, finally, only stepping stones on the path that leads to the Cosmic Guru. The Cosmic Guru – the guru principle of the universe, is at one with Paramashiva, Cosmic Consciousness.

Among the gurus I had, there were some who were not alive on the physical plane. Deeply influenced in my formative years by the life and teachings of Swami Vivekananda, I took him as my guru. I prayed very hard for him to appear and bless me in my dreams, but this never happened. Something else happened instead: when I was praying in the prayer hall of the Ramakrishna Ashram, Sri Ramakrishna appeared vividly in a vision and gave me a meditation mat. He had come to me unsought. Years passed before I could digest this experience.

The next guru also came unsought. Having learnt yoga from Swami Buddhananda, an Australian monk from the Bihar School of Yoga, I started praying for him to become my guru. Whenever we met and I mentioned this desire to him, he would just smile. One evening, when I was meditating and praying intensely in a crowded bus, my yoga teacher's guru, Swami Satyananda, appeared in a vision and touched my third eye chakra.

I did not then know then that what had occurred was my shaktipat. I sat the whole night in deep meditation, and hundreds of doors opened in my third eye chakra. This basically meant that this chakra, which is the seat of intuitive knowledge, had opened.

Swami Satyananda remained my guru for several years, even though I actually met him only twice. After the second meeting, there were many upheavals in my life that brought me much suffering. Eventually, it dawned upon me that these painful experiences were not a coincidence but part of the purification process my guru was putting me through. This was the guru's grace.

When I was being tossed about in the storm, another guru came. Allama Prabhu describes this well:

When the unseen guru
Appears to the eye
The unheard mantra
The untouched touch of the hand
On the head
The invisible linga
The holy shower

From unfilled pots
And an initiation
Unknown to the scriptures.

At another point in my life, there was a guru who started
speaking to me through nadigranthas, divinatory palm
leaf manuscripts. He would first give me an experience
– something would occur in my life – and then give me
an explanation through the palm leaf manuscripts when
I went to the palm leaf reader.

Through the nadigranthas, this guru used to play
fortune teller to ministers and other important people,
who would visit to have their political questions
answered. It was only to me that he started revealing the
mysteries of mantra practice. He shared with me many
mantras that are not found in any text of mantra shastra.
He also revealed to me the power of 'seed syllables', beej
mantra, and how they inform every level of phenomena.
I was taught how to connect to the beej mantra in every
person and object, including the elements and divine
beings. (Every being and every object has a beej mantra
inherent in it.) This guru also taught me the different
orders of mantras, and when and how to use them.

There were other great gurus, living and non-living,
famous and unknown, who came and blessed me
whenever I was stuck. They came to me as teachers,
not as gurus. They included renowned saints like Mata

Amritanandamayi, Baba Virsa Singh, Nirmal Guruji and Yogi Ramsuratkumar, and little-known gurus who belonged to different regions, schools and lineages, such as Shivananda Swami of Pandavpur, Sri Kumar Swamiji of Dharwar, Ramavatar Baba of Kedarnath and Sri Madveereshanatha,

One Sunday morning in 1997, Shivalinga Swami revealed that he had always been my guru, in this life as well as in previous lives. That was a momentous day in my life.

He was a veritable ocean of wisdom. He taught me not just the secrets of mantra shastra but also numerology and different kinds of healing methods, particularly reiki. He often cautioned me about impending dangers in my life, and gave me protection. The close contact and communion with him continued for over fifteen years. After this, as he became more and more a part of my own self, the external dependence with the medium began to lessen.

Shivalinga Swami is still my guru and informs all my experiences at all levels. He is now the light within and without.

Among the living gurus who came to guide me for long periods was my Sufi master, Sheikh Ashad-ullah Quadri Wali Shivayogi. Illiterate but profoundly wise, he came into my life to rid me of my dependence on the intellect. He taught me to think with the heart, and revealed to me the way to akshara, eternal wisdom.

Baba, as I called him, emphasized for me the essence of all things, which was ishq. The paradigm of guru– disciple love, he said, was to be found in the stories of Laila and Manju, Shiva and Parvati, Radha and Krishna. He reminded me time and again that the guru is not a person but a principle pervading everything; it speaks and shines through a million voices and forms if you have the ears to hear and the eyes to see.

His spiritual instruction was through the many stories and anecdotes he shared with me, and his wisdom was conveyed through metaphors. A Lingayat by birth, he had converted to Islam because his guru Akbar Shah Quadri Wali was a Muslim. But Baba did not follow sharia rules, cheerfully smoking ganja and drinking arrack, which he called sura, the drink of the gods. He never went to the mosque but performed what he called the 'dil ka namaz'.

Baba shared his divine knowledge with only a few people. With others who would make their way to his cave in Hebbal on the outskirts of Bengaluru, he feigned ignorance of spiritual matters. In fact, most people who came seeking him would not even manage to reach the cave. He explained to me that not everyone is ready for the inner message from the rishimarg, the path of the sages.

He passed on one day, leaving me after ten years of a very loving bond. I deeply missed his presence in my life. It took me several years to understand that it is the awareness of the guru's all-pervasive presence that makes the guru alive for the disciple; physical life or death has nothing to do with the guru–disciple connection.

Ultimately, it is in the Cosmic Guru as a principle, and not in the guru as a person, that we need to dissolve ourselves.

For the salt in water
The camphor in the flame
Or the disciple in the guru's hands
Is there anything that needs
To be done, O Goggeshwara?

Door 2

MANTRA

THE MANTRA IS NOT ONLY AN IMPORTANT DOOR THAT leads to inner freedom, but is also perhaps the easiest door to enter through in today's times.

Meditation practice, for instance, requires a mind that has already attained a certain level of tranquillity. It also presupposes some level of physical control, for there must be steadiness in the posture if one has to meditate. Unless one has reached an advanced level of meditation, this practice also needs a place and time free from disturbances. Mantra practice, on the other hand, can be done anywhere and at any time.

What is a mantra? An excellent definition of the mantra is 'manaati trayate iti mantrah', 'the mantra is what expands the mind'.

A mantra is a sacred syllable or group of syllables which, if repeated, leads to the expansion of the mental powers of will, knowledge and action.

The will is the ability to make the intent to do something, while knowledge is the information we need to help us perform an action. Will, knowledge and action are unlimited in the case of an awakened yogi, but are present only in a very diminished capacity in an ordinary person. A mantra increases the capacity of a person to will, to take cognizance and to complete an action.

Let me explain how a mantra works. When a person chants a mantra over and over again, the part of the mind that is embroiled in automatic and unwanted thought processes stemming from unfulfilled desires and dissatisfaction with life, is gradually quietened.

In my experience, the practice of a mantra is a sure and safe, albeit slow, method of inner transformation. The mantra works not because it brings awareness or the ability to concentrate but because of the power of repetition. Repetition is the soul of mantra practice; sound energy is its fuel.

The deliberate chanting of the mantra is the first stage of mantra practice. Why I say this is deliberate is because at this point, it is a conscious decision and effort made by the practitioner. Yet, even now, the person does not need to focus his attention on the mantra. Just by chanting, the sound vibrations of the mantra are absorbed into the body, breath and mind until the practitioner reaches a point where the repetition becomes spontaneous.

This stage is now the intermediate stage; here, the distractions of the mind start to become less intense and begin to lose their grip on the practitioner. This is because the part of the mind that tries to distract, consuming a lot of mental energy, is now diverted towards the chanting of the mantra. Gradually, the mantra takes over the mind, and awareness and concentration are spontaneously awakened.

Then, when the distractions cease and the mind attains greater stillness, it becomes connected to the unlimited powers of the cosmic consciousness and attuned to the vibrations of the cosmic mind, which is free from all limitations.

When a person has been chanting a mantra for a while, a part of the mind becomes absorbed in the mantra, but the entire mind is not yet in the mantra. This is an interesting stage in mantra practice, where the part of the practitioner's mind that he does not yet have control over – the arena that is still a storehouse of suppressed fears and desires – becomes a place of great rage and turbulence. This occurs because all that has been hitherto suppressed in the psyche is drawn out by the power of the chanting so it can ultimately be released, and the practitioner healed.

It is at this point that many people, disturbed by the violence in the mind, get frightened and give up the mantra practice. And they fall right back into the vortex, which is actually just a stage, although an essential one, that they have to pass through. If the work is continued, it is this same mantra and its chanting that will also protect the practitioner and take him through the storms raging inside him.

Let me share a parable here to illustrate this. A certain king had many desires, and he wanted them to be fulfilled. When he approached his guru with this request, the guru gave him a ring and told him to wear it. Whenever the king wanted a wish to come true, he had only to twist the ring and a powerful demon would appear to carry out his request. The caveat was that once the demon was summoned, he had to be kept constantly busy with tasks, failing which he would devour the king. The king agreed to this condition.

One day, the king summoned the demon. He made a wish and it was fulfilled for him. Then the demon demanded another task and then another. In this process, all the king's desires were realized until he had nothing more to ask for.

Of course, the demon was now ready to eat him up. The king asked his guru to save him. The guru told him to tell the demon to climb up and down a pillar until the king asked him to stop. The demon began to do so, until he reached a point of total exhaustion. Finally, he begged the king to release him of this task and assured him he would spare his life.

In this parable, the demon is the mind and the pillar is the mantra. The mind has to be used to move beyond the mind, to transcend it and move to a place of no-mind. The mind is finally a tool in your hands: it can serve you or destroy you, depending on how you choose to use it.

In mantra yoga, desires are not enemies that have to be destroyed. But they don't have to be indulged in either, beyond a point. Desires are, in fact, to be acknowledged and then *transcended*. Mantra practice allows this transformation to take place.

Mantras can be simple or complex depending on their length. Some mantras are simple in that they have just one or two syllables like 'Om', 'Hreem' and 'Ram'; others have syllables that range anywhere from three to a thousand in number. The fifteen-syllable Shakta mantra, 'ka e i la hrim/ha sa ka ha la hrim/sa ka la hrim' is one example of a long and complex mantra. This mantra has no rational meaning.

Some mantras have a meaning that can be paraphrased, but others are just sounds. The simplest kind of mantra is nama or the name of the deity, like Ram, Hari and Shiva.

What is common to all mantras is that they are the means of communing with the sonic manifestation of the Cosmic Divine. In other words, mantras work because their sounds embody divine energy. This method is also based on the theory that the whole cosmos emanated from the power of sound. The Cosmic Divine's primary manifestation is sound.

Says the first verse of the Mandukya Upanishad, which is considered the most important of all the Upanishads:

Omityetadakshramivam sarvam
tasyopaanaakhyaanam bhootam bhavishyaaditi
sarvamomkara eva yachchaanya trikaalaateetam
tadapyomkaara.

(Om is one letter, which is all. Everything, past and future, is its elaboration. Nothing other than Om is beyond the three dimensions of time – past, present and future.)

This verse conveys that everything in the cosmos is an emanation of the sound Om, which is the basis of all mantras and is the mantra of mantras.

There are different views regarding the origin of mantras. According to the Vedic tradition, mantras were revealed to sages in deep states of contemplation. The sages blessed with such revelations were called 'mantra dhrshtaras', mantra seers.

The tantric tradition has several stories about the genesis of mantras. According to *Devipurana*, an important tantric text, mantras manifested when Shiva, the Cosmic Self, was copulating with Shakti, Cosmic Energy. During their lovemaking, garlands of skulls worn by Shiva made clanging sounds that caused vibrations in the drum he held in his right hand.

Amused by these sounds, Shakti picked up these sounds to create the 'matrika' (all the sounds that make up the Sanskrit alphabet from 'a' to 'ha'). By putting together the different vowels and consonants of matrika, which represented different deities and energies, she created mantras that would help people realize their wishes, both worldly and otherworldly.

In *Maheshwara Sutra*, a Shaivite text, it is said that fourteen primary mantras emanated from Lord Shiva's drum, and from these fourteen mantras, all other mantras have arisen. The belief among Vaishnavas is that mantras came into being from the sound of Lord Vishnu's conch.

While there are different views on the genesis of mantras, all accounts agree that they are of divine origin and that their purpose is to attain the fundamental human desire – absolute freedom and joy. The following Sanskrit verse, often quoted by mantra yogis, endorses this view:

*Omkaaram bindusamyuktam nityam dhyaayanti
yoginah
Kaamadam mokshadam yasya omkaaraaya namo
namah.*

(Om, which yogis chant daily, is the giver of worldly
benefits and also of moksha. Let us bow down to Om.)

As I have said before, the different doors in this book
lead to one another. The mantra is linked, for example,
to the deity. Mantras are indistinguishable from the
deities that pervade the inner self and the outer world.
Once the seeker has the mantra, he is in direct contact
with the deity. Some yogis go to the extent of saying
that if you have the mantra, you do not need the deity.
Says Purandara Dasa:

Why do I need you or your support?
Is it not enough to have the power of your name?

A mantra is capable of manifesting all the desires of a
person, good or bad, because the cosmic power does
not differentiate between good and bad desires. It was
only after the demon satisfied all the worldly desires of
the king that the king was able to move beyond desire
and grasp the deeper truths waiting for him. In the

same way, the mantra also has the power to take you beyond all longings, to a state of complete bliss and acceptance.

Since a mantra is capable of yielding all goals, it is compared to a priceless diamond. Says Mirabai:

Look! I have got the diamond of the mantra 'Ram'.
Due to his compassion for me, my true guru
Bestowed on me something invaluable.

A well known poet-saint of Maharashtra, Namdev, goes even further. He declares the mantra 'Vithal' to be everything:

Vithal is God and the worship of God
Vithal is the pilgrimage and the pilgrimage site
Vithal is father, mother and guru.

Brahma Chaitanya Maharaj, a famous modern saint of Maharashtra, declared: 'All forms fall away; only the name outlasts all.'

However, a mantra does not only satisfy conscious desires; it also brings to the surface all subconscious desires buried deep within the practitioner's psyche. When I started chanting my mantra, I wanted moksha and that was my resolve. I was surprised to find instead opportunities for fame, wealth and other pleasures coming my way. I had not even been aware that these cravings were hidden in me.

———

Both Buddhism and Jainism are atheistic spiritual traditions, in the sense that they do not believe in a creator or in creation. For them, reality is an eternal existent. Buddhism is wedded to the philosophy of annicha, impermanence. Jainism, on the other hand, bases its cosmic view on the contrast between jiva, eternal consciousness, and ever changing ajiva, matter. Yet, despite being atheistic, both Buddhism and Jainism extol the power of the mantra.

Hinayana Buddhism, based on Pali texts, employs mantras to remind the seeker of the need to surrender to Lord Buddha and his teachings. 'Buddham saranam gachchami', 'let us take refuge in Lord Buddha', is the oft-repeated mantra of surrender. Amida Buddhism in Japan sees mantra recitation as the only path to enlightenment.

There is a whole system in Mahayana Buddhism called mantrayana. Mahayana Buddhism was deeply influenced by Vedic and tantric traditions, where mantras play an important role. In effect, the Mahayana Buddhist schools developed a whole system of mantras based on these traditions. 'Om' was imported into Buddhism from the Vedic tradition.

Mahayana Buddhism also developed an elaborate system of tantric mantras, which bestow on seekers a variety of mundane and spiritual fruits. This is particularly so with Tibetan Buddhism. One of its cardinal mantras is 'Om mani padme hum', which is a mantra to cure all ills, both physical and spiritual. Like most great tantric mantras, this mantra has no rational meaning, and works because of the power of sound.

Like Buddhism, Jainism incorporated the Vedic Om too, but also developed its own complex system of mantras. These mantras focus on surrendering to the full hierarchy of Jain masters. Central to Jainism is the mantra called 'panchanamokara', the five salutations:

Namo arihantaanaam
Namo siddhannam
Namo aahaariyaanaam
Namo uvajjhayanam
Namo loye savva saahunaam.

(I bow down to the liberated ones
I bow down to the adepts
I bow down to masters
I bow down to teachers
I bow down to all saints of the world.)

The shorter form of this mantra is 'namo a-si-aa-u-saa'. Apart from purifying the heart, this mantra is supposed to confer all kinds of blessings. Jainism also developed mantras to appease different classes of deities and heavenly beings.

The science of language holds that the relationship between words, and the meanings ascribed to them, is arbitrary, not natural. It is the result of the way language is formulated. Beyond that, words have no other power. After all, according to science, speech sounds are manifestations of sound, which is a form of matter.

We must turn this view upside down to understand the basics of mantra shastra, which is a spiritual science. Here, spirit or consciousness is the primary reality, not matter. The material world is a gross expression of subtle spiritual phenomena. As Lord Buddha said in the *Dhammapada*, 'mano pubbangama dhamma', 'the mind or consciousness is the foundation of every physical condition'.

Mantra shastra considers the cosmos the manifestation of vak, primordial speech energy, expressing itself through and pervading all dimensions or states of mind: jagrit, wakefulness; swapna, dreaming; sushupti, sleeping; and turiya, the state of unalloyed bliss experienced in the deepest levels of meditation. The cosmos is seen as vagmaya, full of vak.

According to tantric philosophy, the Sanskrit alphabet exists at multiple levels. The alphabet is the matrix of language at all levels. First is the vaikhari level, the level of physical sound, the state of being heard; it belongs to wakeful, everyday consciousness. At a deeper level, it is called pashyanti, half-heard speech, characterizing the dream state. At a still deeper level, in the state of dreamless sleep, it is called para, unheard speech. Below these lies the ultimate source of the above states, paratpara, immanent and transcendental speech energy.

Here, 'a' to 'h', the first and last varnas, speech sounds, represent the first and the last sounds of the Sanskrit alphabet, respectively. The vowels follow 'a', which are then followed by the consonants. The vowels are manifestations of Shiva, and consonants represent Shakti. The vowels and consonants make up the overall field of phonemes or framework, and are combined in units of vak, such as syllables, words, sentences and texts.

This mechanism is expressed in the following Kannada poem by Siddharama:

Vibrations combine with vibrations
And became speech sounds
Sounds combined with sounds
And became words
Words combined with words

And became utterances
Utterances combined with utterances
And became volumes of texts.
Lord Kapila Siddha Mallikarjuna
Is not in vibrations, sounds, words, utterances
Or volumes of texts.

The last sentence states that Lord Kapila Siddha Mallikarjuna, or Lord Shiva, is not present anywhere, because everything is in Him.

The sources of sonic reality are contained in varnas, which are present in the matrika in a specific order beginning with 'a' and ending with 'h'. All knowledge is contained and expressed in the elements of the matrika. Unlike in the modern science of language, these elements of the matrika are not inert sounds but energy units with specific psychic and spiritual properties. Mantras are made up of specific permutations and combinations of varnas. When varnas come together in a specifc order in a mantra, they may or may not carry a rational meaning, but they always carry a psychic and spiritual meaning.

Let us try to understand how mantras are formed. In the matrika, the first sound 'a' is followed by the second 'aa'. Yet, in the greatest mantra of Kashmir Shaivism, the mantra 'aham' violates the sequence by placing the last syllable 'h' next, which in turn is followed by 'm', which is the penultimate sound of the sequence of vowels. This mantra resembles the Sanskrit word 'aham', simply meaning 'I'. This is the rational meaning of 'aham' when it is used as a word in the language.

But the mantra 'aham' has no rational meaning. Instead, it has a symbolic meaning assigned to it in the matrika system. From this perspective, 'a' means the basis of all things. 'H', also called visarga, emission, stands for emanation or creation. 'M', also called bindu, stands for dissolution or destruction. So the symbolic meaning of this mantra points to the whole cosmic cycle from beginning to end at the macro level. The cosmic cycle, according to tantric philosophy, is also contained in the spanda, pulsation, of consciousness at the micro level. The chanting of this mantra activates and enhances all the energies of consciousness and the cosmos.

Now, the wild and whimsical combinations of speech sounds that keep occurring in the mind can influence how we create our experiences. For example, a person can keep telling himself things like 'I am always a loser' or 'the world is a cruel place'. Here, because of this constant repetition, these sounds or thought patterns that also contain energy, start to manifest these messages. Endowed with their own, albeit limited, powers of will, action and knowing, the messages emanating from our subconscious habits and conditioning, start to manifest.

Being possessed by the negative messages, we become their instruments. Though emanating from the highest power, the Cosmic Divine, Paramashiva or Parashakti, the repository of unlimited will, knowing and action, the person forgets his true spiritual identity and associates himself with his psychological or ego identity, which is only a version of his true identity. This is how our world becomes subject to limitations. This principle of limitation is called 'maya' by the tantrics. If we do not watch out, we are easy targets of these terrible powers of the intransigent ego consciousness or ghora shaktis.

These terrible energies can be made benevolent through the mantra. This is because mantras are able to connect the practitioner with the Divine within. Through constant repetition, the practitioner realizes that he is connected to the very source of the matrika, which is the divine self. Contrary to his belief, he is not at the mercy of the wiles of the ego mind. Thus, the mantra effects a spiritual alchemy through which the limiting powers of ego consciousness expand into the unlimited energies of the Cosmic Divine.

Let me now give an account of actual mantra practice. To start with, it is important to choose the right mantra. In the Vedic tradition, it is said that there are seven million mantras in existence. This is because there are are so many kinds of human beings. Different mantras work for different people, and not all mantras work for everyone.

How do we go about finding the right kind of mantra? The greatest mantras are revealed to yogis in the deepest states of spiritual communion. However, since most of us cannot rise to such heights, we need to get mantras from a mantra guru. A mantra guru is one who has realized the power of mantras through intense practice over a long period of time. As a result of attentive repetition, the mantra becomes energized in her consciousness and imbued with mantra veerya, energy of the mantra. It is then that the guru can initiate the disciple into mantra practice.

Every time a mantra is uttered, it becomes more potent and powerful. Through the tradition of mantra gurus, a mantra can be traced back to the rishi to whom it was originally revealed in deeper states of samadhi. The name of the rishi is also invoked before mantra practice so that we can tune in to all the energies of earlier repetitions. Like a river originating from the rishi, the mantra energy flows through whoever works with it. This is the reason why time-tested mantras, having been energized by earlier practitioners, work very quickly.

Unless given by a guru to the disciple through an initiation, a mantra is just sound. The initiation involves the transmission of the mantra energy from the guru to the disciple. Some mantra texts also prescribe a series of preliminary rituals before passing on the mantra. The guru decides which mantra is suitable for the seeker at his present level of spiritual receptivity.

How does one find a mantra guru? My own great guru Shivalinga Swami told me that the guru knows best when to appear. The guru can look deeper into the seeker's heart than the seeker can. Alternatively, if the seeker calls out from the depth of his heart like a helpless child calling out to the mother, the guru can hear it no matter where she is in the cosmos, and responds instantly.

While a guru is the common means to access a mantra, not everyone can find a guru. In this case, one can get the mantra directly from the mantra deity. There have been cases where the deity assumes the role of the guru and initiates the seeker into the mantra in a dream or a vision. A mantra can also arise spontaneously in a seeker in moments of intense emotion, when the ordinary ego mind breaks down.

There are occasions when people get mantras from books, although many experts warn against it because the seeker may not be able to decide what is best for her. But there are also compassionate mantra gurus who make the mantra available for the disciple. Lakshmidhara Acharya, in his commentary on *Soundarya Lahari*, gives to the readers of his text the most deeply hidden mantra of the Shakta tradition. This is the sixteenth and final syllable of the famous panchadashi mantra of the Cosmic Mother. Lakshmidhara Acharya broke the strict rule in the mantra tradition because he considered as a disciple anyone who chose to read his commentary.

There is an endearing story about how Kabir received his mantra initiation. He considered the renowned saint Ramananda his guru. When approached for initiation, Ramananda refused to give a mantra to Kabir as he was a Muslim, but Kabir was determined to get the mantra from him. Ramananda used to go to the Ganga river early every morning to bathe. He had to walk down a flight of steps to reach the ghat. One day, Kabir covered himself and lay down on the steps, and Ramananda inadvertently stepped on him. When this unexpected accident happened, Ramananda exclaimed: 'Ram! Ram!' Kabir repeated these words and considered himself initiated!

Additional elements can be used to invigorate mantra practice. For instance, worshipping the mantra deity is a part of the mantra ritual, and involves offering water, flowers, incense and food to the image of the mantra deity. When the guru gives the mantra to the seeker, she also gives a specific verse that describes the deity associated with the mantra. This deity is the visual embodiment of the mantra, which is easier to connect to than the abstract sound form of the mantra (in the initial stages of work with the mantra).

The chanting of additional mantras and placing the syllables of the mantra on parts of the practitioner's body is also insisted upon.

A yantra is one of the accompaniments of the mantra, and is the abstract visual form of a mantra. Apart from expediting the working of the mantra, a yantra also gives psychic protection to the practitioner from hostile forces. A yantra consists of a combination of geometric figures like triangles, lines, circles and dots.

Different mantras have different yantras. 'Hreem', the seed mantra of Shakti, for instance, has a downward pointing triangle as its yantra. Shiva is represented in the yantra by the opposite image: an upward pointing triangle. The famous Shiva mantra 'Om namah Shivaya' is represented by two interpenetrating triangles, one pointing upwards and the other, downwards. The yantra for the Ganesh mantra 'Gam' is a swastika.

The longer and more complicated the mantra, the more complex the yantra. The sixteen-letter mantra in Srividya tantra is called the Sriyantra, and consists of several interpenetrating triangles embedded in a circle which, in turn, is encased in a rectangle.

Though texts and experts swear by all these rules and prescriptions, we can find actual examples of people for whom mantra practice has worked without such formalism. Further, an accurate pronunciation of mantras is not necessary for the mantra's efficacy. Tradition says that it is sincerity and not self-consciousness about the right form that is the key for mantra sadhana.

The ways of tantra are difficult and demanding. Most tantrik practices require that the disciple have adequate physical strength and prana or breath power. If not, he will not be able to contain the power released by tantric means such as mantra or kriya yoga. For people who need an easier alternative, bhakti provides a good option for spiritual growth.

In devotional bhakti traditions, the intensity and spontaneity of the devotee's love for the deity is the most important thing. Bhaktas flout all rules and call out to the deity with total love. The response comes immediately. Shivalinga Swami once expressed to me the secret of how the mantra works: 'A sincere cry from the heart begins to resonate all through the cosmos.'

I would say that the best technique for mantra practice is one where there is no technique at all. With the heart filled with devotion, if the seeker calls out to the Divine, the mantra works instantaneously no matter how or from where one got the mantra, or what the quality of the chanting is.

There are disciples who chant the mantra simply for the love of the Divine, and make their lives an inexhaustible fountain of joy. All worldly pleasures lose meaning for them. Acharya Utpaladeva, a great Kashmiri saint poet and philosopher says in his *Shivastotravali* (A Garland of Hymns to Shiva):

Shiva ityekakshabdasya jihvaagre tishthatah sada
Samasta vishayaasvaado bhaktaishyevvasti kopaho.

(Those devotees alone on whose tongue forever dwells one word, 'Shiva', experience the joy of all sense-objects put together.)

However, it is also possible to chant mantras for ordinary reasons: to obtain a wish, to ward off danger, to cure an illness, to attain fame and prosperity. In such cases, the seeker knows that the mantra has worked when the specific wish comes true.

I have seen two cases of terminal cancer cured through mantras. I have also seen how wishes manifest. In fact, if you are not chanting a mantra as a pure devotee, it is important to chant with a particular resolve. Else, the energy released by mantra repetition is wasted. The resolve is necessary to channelize the energy generated by the mantra.

Coupled with the direction of the resolve, the mantra energy brings about changes in us and, through us, in the world. In the long run, if practiced steadfastly and with determination in the tantric or bhakti way, the mantra leads us to everlasting bliss and freedom from the shackles of the conditioned mind.

Unlike meditation, the path of the mantra does not require concentration. The practice of chanting can go on even when the mind is not at peace. Once thought-waves recede, thanks to a long period of mantra work, the state of tranquillity arises in the mind spontaneously and meditation happens effortlessly. As Swami Satyananda Saraswati said in a sermon I attended once, as a result of mantra practice we are able to cross the turbulent ocean of the mind without having to understand its nature as we have to do in other practices such as meditation.

At the culmination of the mantra practice, the mantra, devata and guru merge into the practitioner. The realization of the unity of the guru, mantra and devata is the basis of mantra practice and philosophy.

Door 3

DEVATA

DEVATA, THE DEITY, IS ANOTHER CHAMBER THAT A seeker can enter at the start of the spiritual journey or after having experienced inner changes in some other chamber.

The deity is often worshipped in its external form – in the form of an idol, because it is easier for a seeker to seek the Divine in a tangible form. But the deity, in truth, is the divine energy that exists within a person. Just as an artist gives tangible or visible form to inner creative stirrings, the worshipper gives name and form to the inner spiritual energy, and begins to communicate with it.

The relationship between the guru and the disciple often manifests through a mantra which, in turn, is inseparable from the devata. Every mantra is linked to a devata; there is no devata without a mantra. The relationship between the devata and mantra is the same as name and form in everyday experience; one always goes with the other.

In the Judeo-Christian tradition, God is the creator, and essentially beyond all. So, any attempt to embody this formless name is idolatry, and considered disrespectful to the Divine. Indian spiritual approaches to God, such as Shaivism, Vaishnavism, Shaktism, Buddhism and Jainism, are predominantly immanent. Instead of God creating man as in the Judeo-Christian framework, the seeker attributes the human form to his gods.

Of course, when the spiritual experience fructifies, everything is ultimately experienced as divine. But until the time the unruly mind is finally able to experience the all-pervading divine consciousness, it has to be trained to see the Ultimate in a tangible form.

In theistic Indian traditions like Shaivism, Vaishnavism and Shaktism, though the Divine, called by different names such as Paramashiva, Parashakti or Parabrahman, is beyond all forms, we can still communicate with this power through an imagined divine name or form. Such names and forms are handed down by tradition. For instance, Shaivism sees Shiva as the greatest of all beings. He has a formless manifestation as the shivalingam, or as a god with certain attributes: dressed in tiger hide, wearing the moon in his matted hair, holding a trident, drum and torch in his hands.

Some see Shiva as Adiyogi, the primal yogi rapt in deep meditation. Others see him as the loving husband of his divine consort, Parvati, and in myths and in popular imagery, they are sometimes accompanied by their divine sons, Ganesh, the elephant god and Subrahmanya, the warrior god. Shiva is also visualized as Nataraja, the Cosmic Dancer, engaged in the dance of ecstasy. There is a lot of hymnal literature on Shiva to awaken and deepen the practitioner's love for the god. There is also a large body of mythology that depicts and extolls Shiva's sacred deeds.

In Vaishnavism, Vishnu is seen as the highest god. There are some schools of Vaishnavism that see Vishnu as a formless cosmic principle. This is called the nirguna approach. But the more popular schools are the saguna schools, which see Vishnu as an anthropomorphic form, a cosmic being lying on his 'snake bed' in the cosmic ocean with his divine spouse, Lakshmi. Vishnu mythology speaks of his ten avatars. He came down to the earth in human form to save the virtuous and destroy the wicked, and the most important of these avatars are Rama and Krishna. These deities are familiar and beloved in India.

The Shakta school elevates the cosmic feminine as the highest principle. Shakti in her highest manifestation is beyond name or form though she, too, has many different manifestations, for example, as Kali, the dark goddess of time, dancing in fierce abandon upon the corpse of her spouse, Shiva. In her benevolent aspect, she is Tripura Sundari, the greatest beauty of the three worlds, sitting on Shiva's body as visualized in Srividya tantra. In her manifestation as Durga, she quells fierce demons.

Apart from these three major pan-Indian deities and their bewilderingly numerous manifestations, there are other devatas in the regional schools of tantra and bhakti. Murugan/Subrahmanya is a very popular god in Tamil Nadu. Ganesh is adored widely in Maharashtra and other states. Bhairavnath, a fierce attendant of Shiva and Parvati, is loved in the Himalayan region and in the north-western states, while Hanuman is popular all over India.

Ultimately, it does not matter what form of the deity the spiritual practitioner chooses as long as it is one that appeals to her heart and she is able to dwell on it with ease.

Each of these deities is invoked through a major mantra or seed mantras specific to it. As shared earlier, Om namah Shivaya is the most famous of the Shiva mantras. The seed mantra for Shiva is 'Haum'. The best-known Vishnu mantra is 'Om namo Narayanaya'. Vishnu is also worshipped through his seed mantras such as 'Kleem', 'Kreem' and 'Hreem'. Practitioners also use hymns that were composed by ancient sages in order

to invoke individual devatas. These hymns allow them
to commune and communicate with the devata.

God is abstract, impersonal and formless. Devatas,
however, can manifest through three forms: mantra,
yantra and mandala. The mantra is the sound body of
the Divine, while the mandala is the concrete visual body
of the devata as imagined by the mantra practitioner.
The yantra, a visual geometric representation of the
Divine, is the abstract visual body. These methods, being
less tangible than the visual human form, aren't as easy
as relating to a physical form.

Unlike the Judeo-Christian God, which refers to
God as male, the Indian devata can be male, female
or androgynous, although the ultimate godhead in
the Indian traditions is genderless. Depending on the
mantra, the devata can also be a combination of a
human and an animal.

The mantra devatas are as diverse as human
beings and their temperaments. They are the concrete
manifestations of bhavas, the archetypal emotions
that reside deep within us. The devatas are also called
'ishta', our deepest wishes to experience and express
our potential to the hilt.

Since our desires die hard, even after enjoying the
object of yearning, we continue to long for more and
more things. The path of following one's desires can be
an endless journey. However, through spiritual practices,

when we experience firsthand the interconnectedness of everything, the longing for variety ceases.

This happens when the mind is focused on a particular object, which, in this case, is the name or form of the devata.

Contemplation of the devata is meant to help the practitioner remain soaked in the feel and vibrations of the mantra. The repetition of the name and the protracted visualization of the deity will expedite the process of streamlining desires.

In this journey, one moves mostly from the concrete to the abstract. For this to happen, the practitioner should dissolve herself in the form and feel of the devata. This quality of being soaked is called bhavana, which also means 'to feel' or 'to become'. Put another way, the devata becomes the practitioner. This is a stage where mamsapinda, the physical body, becomes mantrapinda, the mantra body.

A conscious dwelling on the visual image of the deity is an active and purposive cultivation of the power of the imagination to transform things by channelizing the power of visualization. Otherwise, the mind is distracted by a deluge of unwanted images and thoughts.

The devata one chooses usually resonates with one's own emotional nature. Devatas can be visualized in their benevolent or malevolent aspect depending on what emotion is predominant in the practitoner. It is better for a mind consisting largely of fear to focus on the mantra of a fearful devata like Kali or Bhairav. If, on the other hand, one has a greater propensity for that which is beautiful, the mantras of benevolent devatas like Krishna or Lakshmi are useful.

The devatas whom we invoke will finally lead us to freedom from all inner limitations. But they can also be invoked to satisfy our mundane desires, like curing an illness or creating greater prosperity and happiness for ourselves and others.

The tantric approach to the devata may have various objectives, mundane and spiritual, but the worship of the deity in the bhakti tradition has no other objective than the love of the Divine. The joy of being in love surpasses the desire for all other powers and pleasures. My own mahaguru has taught me that the bhakti way of approaching the deity is easy and full of joy.

In bhakti, the name *is* the form. For example, the name 'Ram' is considered superior to the form of the deity. Just his name carries all the power the practitioner needs to connect to his divinity.

In bhakti, the relationship between the deity and the devotee is not based on any rules of give and take. The devata can send his grace to the devotee at any time without any preconditions. As is the case with unconditional love, the true bhakta does not complain, no matter what the devata inflicts upon her. For her, nothing is sweeter and more satisfying than the joy of calling upon the Divine. She is filled with joy and rid of all anguish the moment she begins to utter the name of the devata.

The yogi and the tantric have to perform the most difficult practices to attain enlightenment. Tantrics have to tame the body, breath and mind. Without strict discipline they may slip and fall into the conditioned state of mind. Constant vigilance is a price they must pay. The bhakta, on the other hand, sings and dances the name of the Divine in pure abandon. Basavanna writes:

I do not know the rules of playing music
I do not know the counts and beats
I do not know the meter and measure
Because nothing can be taken away from You
I sing as I please.

This is a declaration of the bhakta's freedom from the demands of rigorous training and practice. Sometimes, this freedom from rules is experienced as grace. Like a child receiving unconditional love from the mother, the bhakta receives all as well. Akka Mahadevi suggests that effortlessness is the ultimate path:

Can I please you with eight types of worship?
You are far away from all

External observances.
Can I please you with chanting and singing?
You are beyond words.
Can I please you
With concentration and meditation?
You are beyond the mind.
Can I hide you in the heart-lotus?
You inform everything.
It is beyond me
To please you.
Be pleased yourself,
O Chennamallikarjuna.

In one of the most intense periods of my own practice of Shakta (Devi) mantras, I went to the Adishakti temple near Chennai and meditated all day for a whole week. I wanted the Divine Mother to reveal to me the most sacred and secret seed syllable of the Shakta mantra. No revelation came, but on the last day, Mother whispered in my ears:

If you want to reach me through the tantric
practice,
I will be very strict with you, like a headmistress.
But if you call out to me like a child calling out to a
mother,
You will have all my love and care.

Door 4

KAYA

WHAT SHALL WE DO WITH THE KAYA, BODY, DURING our spiritual journey? There are conflicting views on the use of the body in the Indian spiritual traditions.

One view advocates taming, controlling and, finally, renouncing the body. The ascetic traditions of Jainism, Buddhism and some streams within the Shaivite, Vaishnavite and Shakta schools believe the body to be a limitation on the spiritual path. This view also perceives the body to be a trap because it ties one down to the material world.

Thus, ascetics rein in the body and the senses by gradually curtailing their involvement in life. They do this by bruising the body. Pain is used to turn the practitioner away from the pleasurable aspects of the senses. Says Kaivara Naranappa, an eighteenth-century mystic poet from Karnataka:

Come, O Father, Govinda
Rid me of the bondage of birth
I am tired and sick of dragging
Along this body's carriage.

The Jain practice of yoga is a case in point. This path
of achieving spiritual freedom involves not just turning
away from all temptations of the flesh but renouncing
the body. The Jains believe that the body is a source
of danger on the spiritual path. This was summed up
by the eleventh-century Jain poet, Janna, in his work
Yashodhara Cherite:

However many dangers there are
For all of them the body is the home.
Whoever trusts this body cannot help
Searching for Madu fruit in the desert.

Jain monks train the body to get adjusted to more and
more discomfort. Even during initiation, the initiate's
hair is pulled out one by one. I have witnessed this
excruciating process myself. The endurance of pain
is the first test the initiate goes through. All pleasures
and even basic comforts are shunned on this path. For
example, Shvetambara Jain monks wear only white
garments and Digambara Jain monks remain naked,
although women initiated into the Digambara sect are
allowed to wear white clothes.

Jain monks have to live on alms offered by devotees. Alms are put into cupped hands, for the monks are not allowed to use plates or cups. Traditionally, in both Jain sects, the body is denied even the act of bathing, and also the comforts of a bed. The Shwetambara sect has modified things a little; for example, their monks eat from simple plates.

Bound by a firm vow to practise non-violence, Jain monks have to ensure that no harm is caused to even the tiniest insects. Hence, while walking, sitting or sleeping, they sweep the floor with a broomstick to keep insects out of their way. They cover their noses with a piece of cloth to ensure they don't breathe in and kill tiny organisms.

The most courageous of Jain monks eventually renounce life, first giving up solid food and then liquids. Having learned to live purely on air, they gradually abandon their bodies. This is the ultimate sadhana, and thousands of Jains have achieved this feat. The vicinity of Shravanabelagola, the well-known Jain pilgrimage centre in Karnataka where Bahubali, the biggest monolithic statue in the world stands, is littered with nishidige stones. Nishidige stones are memorial stones erected to commemorate a Jain monk or a lay follower who has performed a sacred death rite and given up his body.

This Jain path of consciously taming the body in order to transcend it is definitely a time-tested and efficient means of liberation. Even today, there are innumerable Jain seekers who undergo excruciating hardships to attain inner purity.

Other ascetic schools, along with following the austerities mentioned above, also participate in practices like meditating standing on one leg and observing the vow of silence. Still, whatever methods an ascetic chooses to tame the body, the intent remains the same: to free oneself from the body and the senses.

At the other extreme is the path of vamachara or left-handed tantra. Its techniques are based on breaking taboos imposed by conventional ascetic ethics. Here, having sex, eating meat and drinking alcohol, for example, are used as a *part* of the spiritual practice, and become tools to transform the body into a receptacle for the Divine. These tantrics believe that the body can be used as an instrument to awaken the Divine within.

Long before modern psychiatry arrived, the ancient tantrics had realized the inescapable power of desire and sexuality, the source of our bondage to the limited, physical self. But, just as body can be the home of sickness as well as the fountainhead of joy, sexuality can also be used as freedom from bondage. And that is how they utilized the body as a tool in their spiritual journey.

These tantrics also used methods such as asanas, pranayamas and the practice of bandhas (contractions of muscles in the pelvic area, stomach and throat). Breathing techniques increase the body's vitality, while bandhas train one to hold the breath and sexual emission for as long as is required. The techniques of the vajroli mudra (contraction of the uro-genital canal), ashwini mudra (contraction of anal muscles) and moola bandha (contraction of the vestigial and perineal glands), need to be perfected before someone can be initiated into tantric sex rites.

Sex is important in tantra because sexual energy is directed to the higher chakras so that it can be transmuted into spiritual energy. Tantrics do not spend or release their sexual energy. Tantra uses and intensifies physical pleasures, but only in order to spiritualize them.

Thus, in tantric practice, panchamakara sadhana or the ritual of the five 'Ms' – all the pleasure objects shunned by the ascetics – are employed. These include madya, wine; mamsa, meat; matsya, fish; mudra, parched grain; and maithun, sexual intercourse.

Dakshinachara or right-handed tantra aims at spiritualizing the body without the use of the elements employed in vamachara tantra. This works for people who are not temperamentally suited to sex, alcohol and other pleasures of the body. Their aim is the same as that of the vamachara tantrics – the union of Shiva and Shakti; however, this union happens within the practitioner and not with the aid of a sexual partner, as occurs in the vamachara branch. The Shiva and Shakti energies, or the male and female energies, are located within the body and used to effect the same union.

The kundalini in the chakra at the base of the spine is associated with the Shakti energy while the crown chakra above the head is linked with the Shiva energy. These polarities are used for the Shiva–Shakti union in dakshinachara tantra. Hatha yoga is also used by tantrics to balance and unite the Shiva and Shakti energies within one's own body.

Thus, both the left-handed tantra and right-handed tantra are body-centred schools, and tantra embraces and transforms physical desires into spiritual strengths.

Yogic practices can also increase the physical energies of the body and heighten its vibrational levels. This is what hatha yoga texts like *Hatha Yoga Pradipika* mean when they say that mastering hatha yoga techniques make one seductive like Kamadeva, the love god.

Therefore, the body cannot be eschewed on the spiritual path. Whether one denies it or uses it, it has to be acknowledged, for it is a powerful instrument. The adage popular with yogis is 'shareeramaadyam khalu dharma saadhanam', 'the body is the means of achieving the spiritual goal'. Kabir says, 'Is ghat antar baagbageeche', 'inside this body are gardens.'

Let me now explain the concept of detachment in the context of the body. Whichever path is adopted by a practitioner, detachment is very much a part of the process. Tantrics, for example, use the body in profound ways, but they still need to be detached from it to ensure that the body does not use *them*. Their detachment lies in their conscious use and channeling of the body's energies for a higher purpose.

With ascetics, detachment from the body is more obvious, but here too, they are very conscious of the body while learning to tame it. The path of obvious detachment followed by ascetics is suitable for people who have either attained satiety in terms of the physical senses or are by nature uninterested in the world of the senses.

An important principle underlying yogic physiology is the correspondence between pindanda, the physical body, which is considered to be a micro-cosmos, and brahmanda, cosmos. This correspondence between the two is the basis of spiritual practice and philosophy. 'As above, so below' is the cardinal principle of spirituality the world over.

According to the spiritual philosophy of correspondence, both the human body and the cosmos consist of five elements: earth, water, fire, air and ether.

In the yogic view, these correspond to different parts of the human body. The earth occupies the region between the toes and the knees. Water spreads between the knees and the navel. Fire is located between the navel and the chest. Wind is situated between the chest and the eyebrow centre. Ether is located between the eyebrow centre and the crown of the head. The cosmos is also constituted by the same elements. Each element is associated with the chakras in the human body.

By purifying the elements within the body, one is able to purify the same elements externally; the reverse is also true. Impurities occur in people due to the imbalance of elements within the body. For example, if the water element is overactive, the body becomes phlegmatic; if the fire element is overactive, the person is excessively restless. If the fire element is underactive, on the other hand, the person becomes inactive and lazy.

When one practices yoga, these defilements, which lead to illnesses both physical and mental, are purified. Thus, by making friends with the elements within the body, a yogi is able to establish harmony with the elements outside.

Yogi Veeram Nath, an Aghori baba I met in Lunawada in Gujarat in the early nineties, made this principle clear to me in a telling way. 'You are a wise man,' he said. 'Tell me what the distance is between the earth and the sky?' I said, 'Who can measure that immense distance?' Veeram Nath replied, 'It is only six feet.' 'How?' I questioned. He replied: 'That is the approximate distance between your feet and head. Your feet constitute the earth element and the head the sky. In between are the other elements: water, fire and air. Our Lord Aghora Shiva dwells in all of them.' He then chanted an Aghori mantra:

Aghor aghor prithvi aghor
Aghor aghor pani aghor
Aghor aghor agni aghor
Aghor aghor vayu aghor
Aghor aghor akash aghor.

(Aghor is that which is sweet. All the elements are manifestions of aghor, and they feed on each other.)

Yogic practices like hatha yoga and tantric practices like panchamakara sadhana, which employ 'forbidden' things, as explained above, are meant to wake up the dormant earth energy in the base chakra and then take it up through the intervening chakras. These chakras correspond to the elements of earth (base chakra), water (pelvic chakra), fire (navel chakra), air (heart chakra) and ether (throat chakra). The goal is to take the kundalini energy to the crown chakra located above the head.

Once the kundalini energy is aroused, it has to be conducted through the sushumna nadi, the central psychic passage. Nadis are the subtle canals in the body through which prana, life force, flows. There are many nadis in the body, but the most important ones are the ida nadi, corresponding to the breath in the left nostril; the pingala nadi, corresponding to the breath in the right nostril; and the sushumna nadi, the central breath flowing along spinal column. The balance between the ida and the pingala needs to be attained to make the sushumna active. It is when the breath and consciousness flow through the sushumna nadi that one enters deep states of awareness.

When a person starts his spiritual journey, he needs to undergo some kind of cleansing process that will allow for inner as well as physical purification. For instance, he can undertake hatha yoga kriyas like neti or the purification of the nadis through breath practices. In any hatha yoga practice, one has to cleanse the other nadis to open the sushumna nadi for the vital energy to flow through. If this is not done, the energy may go into the left or right nadi when the kundalini arises. If this occurs, it could result in madness or even death.

As I have explained earlier, in the tantric view of the world, just as the body is a microcosm, the world is the macrocosm, and each is mapped on the other. While working on the body, the external world is also impacted.

Let me explain how this is so. The purification of the body through yogic and tantric practices results in the purification of the mind. Once greater clarity and tranquillity of mind are achieved, the intuition becomes sharper. This helps one think, speak and act without being guided by the impulsiveness of the conditioned body–mind. When actions are freed from conditioning and actuated by the Self, they are bound to influence the external world. Awakened yogis transform the world through their state of inner joy and freedom because these are the energies they transmit.

The story of the great sage Vishwamitra is a case in point. Thanks to his intense practice of austerities, he gained so much power that the gods became jealous of him. They sent the heavenly damsel Menaka to tempt him out of his state of absorption. The moment the sage opened his eyes, he was completely consumed by Menaka's bewitching charms. Forgetting his spiritual practice, he began to drink deep from the cup of erotic pleasures till his daughter, Shakuntala, was born. He then understood that he had strayed from the path, and went back to his spiritual practice. However, by this time, much of the spiritual merit he had accumulated had been spent.

Vishwamitra is one of the 'seven sages' in Indian mythology. His story illustrates the tension between the demands of the body and the spirit. Yet, the other six sages – Jamadagni, Bharadwaja, Gautama, Atri, Vashishtha and Kashyapa, did not experience this kind of tension. They led happy married lives along with their spouses – Renuka, Susheela, Ahalya, Anusuya, Arundhati and Aditi, respectively. They did not see their wives as hindrances but as companions on the spiritual path. The women served their husbands with dedication, helped maintain the ashrams, looked after the disciples and practiced sadhana themselves. Their adherence to pativratya, desiring no man other than the husband, even mentally, bestowed on them enormous spiritual powers.

What I am trying to convey through the example of these sages is that the body can be either a block or an aid to spiritual practice, depending on one's approach to sadhana.

What path shall one choose in the modern world? This is a very personal decision, and one has to make a choice after listening to one's heart. A person who cannot detach from worldly pleasures can adopt the tantric path, while those who are more detached can adopt a path more ascetic in nature.

Having said this, there is nothing wrong even when one makes a choice that turns out to be incorrect or inappropriate, like Siddhartha does in Herman Hesse's fictional work, *Siddhartha*. He takes to the path of renunciation and soon discovers that it does not suit him. He then wills the opposite: a life of utter sensuality. Kamala, a courtesan trained in the erotic arts, takes him through an intense sexual journey. And then, what he could not attain through renunciation, he attains through the path of active engagement in the world of the senses because, once he is satiated, he is able to move beyond his desires.

If you reach one extreme, there is nowhere to go except in the opposite direction. In Jinasenacharya's *Poorvapurana*, Adinath, the first of the liberated beings in the Jain pantheon, experiences a surfeit of sexual pleasures in life after life. In his last human birth, he establishes his imperial power all over the world. It is only after all this that he perceives the transience of all things.

The spiritual journey is more about training and fine-tuning the body, either through direct involvement or through detachment. The point is that the body should not be negated; it has to be engaged with, and there is no escape from it on the spiritual path.

Even asceticism is only a phase and not the complete journey. It is often described as a pilgrim's progress though the inner landscapes of the body. This is what is beautifully depicted in many yogic songs like

the following one by Sarpabhushana Shivayogi of
Karnataka. Here, the body is praised as the sacred hill
of Srigiri, the mythical abode of yogis and siddhas:

I have been to Srigiri
The place of pilgrimage
Srigiri is inside the body
Om Sri Gurusiddha
Yogis know a secret road.

Having walked through seven hills
I plunged into three valleys
I soared up to Kailasa's doors
Om Sri Gurusiddha
And found the southern temple.

Inside the seven-walled fort
Between long staircases
Cymbals, drums and bells
Om Sri Gurusiddha
Beat from time to time.

After the nine doors
Are set four streets
With seven ponds overflowing
Om Sri Gurusiddha
Two pillars and a peak.

Having bathed in nether waters
I climbed up the king of peaks
And gazed at the linga of light
Om Sri Gurusiddha
The linga of light on the palm.

Quelling eight obstructing bulls
I stopped six old tigers
And trampled down the roaring serpent's hood
Om Sri Gurusiddha
I tied down the wandering monkey.

Having crossed the confluence
Of seven sacred rivers
Reached the hidden plantain groves
And entered the lonely cave
Om Sri Gurusiddha
I saw the seven-coloured linga.

The sun rising in Indra's land
Set in Chandra's city
Beautiful colours appeared
Om Sri Gurusiddha
I paused to see it as void.

To the south-east of the peak
Behind Arkrswara's temple

Five immortal waterfalls
Om Sri Gurusiddha
No death after drinking it.

Thus, Srishaila's splendours
I saw beyond illusions
And entered the inner temple
Om Sri Gurusiddha
You had become the tranquil one
Lord Mallikarjuna.

While appearing to describe the pilgrimage to the Shaivite shrine of Mallikarjuna in the hills of Srishaila/ Srigiri, the poem actually depicts the yogi's secret journey through the fascinating landscape of the body.

Door 5

PRANA

PRANA IS BREATH ENERGY. IF BREATH IS THE EXPRESSION of prana, prana is the essence of breath. Breath is the gross manifestation; prana is the subtle principle.

Prana connects breath with the life force that pervades all of life and the cosmos. This life force has different names in different cultures. In China, it is called 'chi'. The cosmic healing power used in Japanese reiki is 'ki', also a manifestation of prana.

Of all that is tangible in the world around us, our bodies are primary. From the time we are born, we start relating to the world around us through our bodies. How we experience our bodies impacts the way we experience the world; the opposite is also true. Most people are aware of the body and, to a lesser extent, the mind, but they are hardly ever aware of the breath.

The experience of the body is incomplete without the mind. The mind interprets experience, labeling it as 'good', 'bad', 'pleasant' or 'unpleasant'. Beyond the mind, we assume another level of subjective reality – consciousness, which is most often referred to as 'atman'. Mind and consciousness are hard to grasp because they are not directly accessible to our senses. As we move from body to mind, we move from a primarily physical and objective entity towards a predominantly non-physical and subjective plane of being.

Between body and mind, there is another level of reality that keeps body and mind together. This is the bridge between the physical body and non-physical mind. This is breath. Breath is coeval with life. We start breathing the moment we are born, and stop breathing when we die. Breath is subtler than body but gross as compared to the atman.

In yoga, the practices of hatha yoga and raja yoga begin with the body, but whether we begin yoga with the body or the breath, these physical or breathing practices are finally spiritual in nature; they all aim to free the practitioner from conditioning.

Body, breath and mind are interconnected, and thus they impact each other all the time. When the body is relaxed, the breath is deep, slow and rhythmic. When the body is restless, the breath is short and shallow. The mental state also reflects the state of the body. If the body is relaxed, the breath is also relaxed, and this, in turn, calms the mind. When the mind is calm, the body and the breath will be calm as well.

When our mind is extroverted or focused on external objects or actions, we function more on the physical plane. When we are deeply absorbed in thought or emotion, our bodily existence becomes subservient to the inner process. The in-between subjective reality is breath, poised between body and mind.

Even after one establishes a considerable degree of control over the body through physical methods like asanas and bandhas, the mind defies control to a large extent unless we take control of the breath. To enter the deepest states of tranquillity – essential for inner awakening – our breath needs to be trained. When the breath is restless, we cannot reach the stages of deeper awareness.

Just as the body is the doorway to the breath, the breath is the doorway to the mind. The experience of yogis has proved that it is much easier to handle the intractable mind once we learn to manage breath. It is for this reason that yogis have evolved different techniques to make friends with and harness the breath.

In the yogic sciences, working on breath opens for us deeper dimensions of prana. The practices that operate at the level of breath are called 'pranayama'. One of the meanings of this Sanskrit word is breath control, and this is how it is usually understood. However, one of my gurus, Swami Satyananda Saraswati, emphasized another aspect of the word. According to him, the word 'pranayama' is made of two words 'prana' and 'ayama', where ayama means 'dimensions'. Therefore, pranayama is not just breath control; it also means becoming conscious of the different dimensions of the flow of breath: inhalation, exhalation and retention.

Yogic negotiations with breath have two aspects: breath control and breath awareness. Breath control involves a conscious and rhythmic lengthening or shortening of the inhalation, exhalation and retention of breath. Breath awareness methods ask that we become conscious of the phases of breath without active intervention. The hatha yoga and raja yoga approaches emphasize active breath control, while the Buddhist schools and some tantric schools recommend a passive watching of the breath and its phases.

Hatha Yoga Pradipika, the classic manual of hatha yoga, cautions practitioners and says that pranayama practice is as risky as playing with a tiger. Many experts advise us not to take to pranayama without the constant guidance of a qualified guru. They say that mistakes in practice may not only bring about the opposite of the promised benefits, but may even cause madness or death. These fears, however, are often exaggerated.

But, at the same time, pranayama calls for care and discipline because if you use the breath incorrectly, for example, holding it for too long, it can impact the heart and blood pressure.

Though there are different types of pranayama, all of them recognize four phases: in-breath, holding within, out-breath and holding without. The holding in is the conscious extension of pauses between breathing in and out. All these phases are present in regular breathing but in regular breathing, this is usually without rhythm because there is no awareness or conscious training of the breath. The techniques of pranayama set out to bring rhythm and harmony to the phases of breathing by introducing a certain kind of ratio between the different phases of breathing.

When the breath moves, the mind moves. When the breath stops, the mind stops. When the breath is stilled, thoughts die down. When the breath begins to move again, thoughts arise again. All of us can observe first-hand that when the mind is in a deeply reflective stage, the breath slows down. In the deepest states of contemplation, the breath temporarily comes to a standstill. Like the surface of the pond reflecting the direction and speed of wind, the breath reflects whatever the mind feels.

By the same token, it is possible to make the mind move in a certain direction or stop it altogether by moving or stopping breath. It is much easier to influence the mind through breath than the other way around because breath is the grosser of the two.

Unlike other breathing exercises, yogic techniques use breath to direct prana. Yogic pranayama techniques, like any other yogic practice, are meant to balance opposites: in-breath and out-breath; internal and external retentions.

No less important is the balance between the 'right' and 'left' breaths. The breath through the left nostril is identified with the ida nadi, and the breath through the right nostril is identified with the pingala nadi. As I have explained earlier, prana flows in subtle energy channels that run through the body, unlike gross breath.

The ida nadi is also called the moon nadi as the breath corresponding to it, issuing from the left nostril, is cooler than that coming from the right nostril. The pingala nadi is called the sun nadi as the corresponding breath flow from the right nostril is warm.

Ida and pingala have diametrically opposite properties. Ida represents the feminine aspect, intuition, imagination, emotion, the arts and introversion. Pingala represents the masculine aspect, reason, conceptualization, intellect, science and extroversion. A balance between these two sets of properties is essential for the optimal functioning of the human mind. The dynamic balance between the two is represented by the sushumna nadi.

Swara yoga is another kind of breath-based yoga. The science of swara yoga has developed highly elaborate techniques of taking advantage of the polarity between ida and pingala. At any given point of time, only one of the three nadis is more active than the other. Ida and the pingala dominate in turns, and each reigns for approximately forty minutes. When neither is dominant in the period in between, which lasts a few seconds, sushumna takes over.

When the right breath (associated with the pingala nadi) is predominant, the mind is active and drawn to the outside world; when the left breath (associated with the ida nadi) takes over, it causes the mind to focus on inner states like fear, anger and hope. Hence, the pingala flow facilitates extroverted actions like manual/physical work, while the ida flow makes it easy to engage in introverted activities like reflection, planning and creative writing.

Swara yoga teaches us how to use all this information for our benefit. It is easy to check which breath is flowing at any moment by bringing your fingers close to your nostrils. Now, for example, if you want to engage in an introverted activity, check which nostril the breath is flowing from. If it is the left one, you can postpone your external activity till the right breath becomes active.

Or else, you can use one of the techniques meant to stimulate the other breath.

The simplest way to change the channel of the breath from the left to the right nostril is to press the soft spot in the left armpit between the bones for a little while; this will open the right nostril. The left breath flow can be activated by reversing this and pressing the soft spot in the right armpit. We can also achieve this by sleeping on the side opposite to the breath to be activated. The right flow controls the left part of the body, and the left flow controls the right.

The over-activity and under-activity of the ida and pingala have several implications for physical and mental health. For instance those with an overactive ida are prone to illnesses stemming from the paucity of heat in the body: excessive phlegm, breathing disorders or constipation. On the other hand, those with an excessive pingala flow are vulnerable to heat-related illnesses like hypertension, acidity and insomnia. Most people who have a problem with phlegm tend to sleep on their right side, which makes the left breath active all night. If people with such problems start sleeping on the left side, this will go a long way in curing the excess of phlegm.

These flows impact mental health as well. Too much ida tends to make us lethargic, depressive and timid.

Excessive pingala makes us impatient, restless, impulsive and short-tempered. Such imbalances can be offset with a conscious management of the dominant breath flow. Also, when one devotes oneself to spiritual practices like yoga, meditation or prayer, thoughts slow down and become manageable.

As I have shared elsewhere, the traditional Indian world view believes that the world within and without are made of the five elements: earth, water, fire, wind and ether. Good health and harmony are possible if, through meditative awareness, we can make the breath associated with a certain element flow through both nostrils. Swara yoga uses the breath to balance and harmonize the elements within the body.

Within the nostril, each element has a fixed physical route through which it flows in and out. Within both nostrils, the breath representing the same element should be flowing at the same time. If different elements are being triggered at the same time, then there is an imbalance, resulting in disharmony at the physical and mental levels. For instance, if the breath pertaining to the earth element is flowing into one nostril and the breath representing the water element is flowing through the other nostril, there will be an imbalance. Swara yoga teaches us to become conscious of the relationship between the breath and the elements. Swara yoga techniques make it possible for us to activate at will whichever breath flow is helpful to what we want to do with ourselves and the world.

Both swara yoga and pranayama are based on the same principles of ida and pingala polarity, but their techniques are different. Swara yoga uses meditative awareness and visualization as tools of transformation. As suggested earlier, pranayama involves an active intervention and a programming of the breath.

The most important aspect of pranayama practice is the purification of the nadis through alternate nostril breathing. At the psychic level, it opens the path of the sushumna nadi, along which the kundalini energy can travel unhindered from the base chakra to the top chakra. At the psychological level, it balances extroversion and introversion. At the physical level, it gives us a feeling of lightness.

There are two other pranayamas I would like to talk about, which involve alternate nostril breathing. Suryabedha pranayama is a method where rhythmic breathing is done by breathing in from the right nostril and breathing out through the left. By activating the pingala nadi, it creates warmth in the body and wakes up the sluggish mind. If we reverse this, breathing in from the left and out through the right, this cools down the body and calms the mind. This is called chandrabedha pranayama and it activates the ida nadi.

Kapalabhati and bhrastrika, two other types of pranayama prescribed in hatha yoga texts, have the effect of purifying the body of excess phlegm and toxins, and freeing the mind from distractions. Kapalabhati means 'cleansing of the skull' and involves forceful and conscious exhalation and spontaneous inhalation. Bhrastrika means 'bellow breath'. It requires us to breathe in and out consciously and forcefully.

Sitali and sitkari are pranayamas that cool down the body and combat thirst, hunger and fatigue. Both of them involve breathing in through the mouth and breathing out through the nostrils. In sitali, we suck the air in by rolling the tongue like a pipe. In sitkari, we suck the air in through the teeth.

Therefore pranayama, as is clear from the brief discussion above, can balance the opposites of body and mind such as heat and cold, effort and relaxation, extroversion and introversion.

Though the exercises I have talked about ask for actively taking charge of the breath, they do not suggest anything harsh or extreme where one's breathing is concerned as they are making the most of what breath normally does. Doing them forcefully is inimical to the spirit of yoga. When breath is treated forcefully in some way, it becomes an enemy to be conquered, and that is not the right attitude or method at all. Further, it may lead to a breakdown in health if handled roughly.

My own pranayama teacher, Swami Buddhananda, instructed us to treat the breath like we treat our beloved, which means that we should play with the breath tenderly like a lover and not treat it like a demon to be conquered!

It needs to be stressed that the pranayamas discussed above, where we consciously superimpose rhythmic patterns on the stages of the breath, are not the only breath practices known to yogis. Since pranayama is about the discovery of the hidden dimensions of the breath, the techniques of observing breath passively without any conscious interference are equally important. In fact, this is the basic practice in Buddhist traditions.

In the Buddhist system of meditation based on sati, awareness, pride of place is accorded to breath meditation. Anapanasati, mindful watching of breath coming in and going out, is the essence of this system. It is said in the Buddhist tradition that the simplest way to enlightenment is watching every breath for a whole day and night. This is not easy at all, because the mind begins to wander soon enough. The practice of anapanasati leads to equanimity, which in turn results in the emergence of vipassana, spiritual intuition.

Unlike pranayama, breath awareness does not involve conscious control like the shortening, lengthening or holding of breath; it is the very act of applying

Door 6

MANA

MANA, MIND, IS A CHAMBER THAT IS USUALLY EXPLORED much later on the spiritual path, for working on and with the mind is not an easy task. Though we are working through the mind all the time, it is not concrete or tangible like the body or breath, which makes it difficult for us to work with.

Therefore, many spiritual seekers find it easier to start their sadhana with the body or breath. We can touch and feel our bodies; we can feel and do things with our breath consciously, even though breathing is spontaneous.

Ideally, yoga has to be practised simultaneously on three planes: body, breath and mind. Yoga is based on the interconnectedness of these three planes, and also reinforces the unity of these planes. Even physical practices like yogic postures do not yield optimum results if done only at the physical level. What I mean by this is that even in doing asanas, the breath has to be used consciously and the mind has to be aware of what is going on in the body and with the breath. To benefit from breath practices, the relaxation of the body and consciousness is a must.

As the sadhana progresses, one moves increasingly from body to mind. When the body's awareness, through asanas and other physical methods, becomes developed, then the attention moves to the breath. When breath, over time, becomes rhythmic and relaxed, then the awareness shifts to the mind.

Let us first understand the Indian spiritual concept of mind. The traditional Indian view is fundamentally different from the Western concept of mind as well as from our general everyday understanding of what the mind is.

Most of us feel that the mind we 'think' with is inside us, whereas the world where things exist and where we 'do' things is outside us. In other words, the mind is subjective reality while the world consisting of matter is objective. Atheists and agnostics experience the mind within the body and the material world outside the body, with the body as something in between. According to scientific materialism, however, everything inside and outside us is matter, except that the mind is a more evolved form of matter. Theistic religions believe that there is an everlasting soul and an absolute God.

We are always trying to improve the mind with the mind, and we hit a dead end again and again. The mind, with most of us, does the opposite of what we ask it to do: the more we try to control it, the more it misbehaves. To escape from the intransigent mind and feel anchored in the endless flux of mental events, we depend on selective memories, impressions and experiences of the past to help us construct the sense of 'I'. But, sooner or later, suppressed fears and anxieties within us erupt and come to the surface.

The Sanskrit equivalent of the mind is 'chitta', though in most Indian languages today, 'mind' is translated as 'mana'. In Sanskrit, chitta and mana are sometimes used equivalently, but chitta is more comprehensive than mana in Patanjali's yoga system. In his sankhya yoga system he explains chitta in a simple way. According to him, it is a composite phenomenon made up of the following parts:

- Mana, the door through which sensations of the external world are received.
- Buddhi, the faculty that gives recognition to things in the world around us.
- Ahankara, the 'I' or the ego, which is the focal point of all our mental activity.

Together, with these constituents, chitta is called 'antahkarana', the inner sense organ. Patanjali defines yoga as the cessation of the fluctuations of chitta: chitta has to be stilled.

If we have only chitta and the external world, no experience can happen because neither of them is sentient. We understand and experience the inner and outer worlds only when they are lit up, as it were, by the light of a conscious intelligence within us, and this is called Purusha.

Purusha is the animating principle which, with Prakriti, gives rise to the material universe. It is also the consciousness within, by virtue of which we understand things and the processes of Prakriti or the changing principle. Purusha is the still centre of the changing world; by itself it is inactive but because of it everything becomes active.

In the Shwetashvottara Upanishad, it is written:

Shrinvantu vishve amritasya putraa
Arya dhamani divyani thasthu
Vedam ayetam purusham mahantam
Aditya varnam tamasa parastath.

(Listen to me, O children of Immortality, I have seen something sacred, I have seen and sensed Great Purusha, the inner sun beyond the darkness.)

It is the presence of Purusha that makes us understand inner and outer events and movements. This entity is the eternal part of us, and is given names such as 'atman' in Vedanta and tantric philosophy, and 'jiva' in Jainism.

Spiritual practice, according to Vedanta and Patanjali, helps us turn away from the snare of the senses and the lures of chitta, both of which are in constant flux. This is done through identification with Purusha. Purusha is the unchanging core of the self. Dualistic schools of tantra such as Pashupata or Tamil Shaivism also adopt the same approach to sadhana as does Patanjali.

Monistic tantras like Kashmir Shaivism or Srividya have a different approach. They believe that the ultimate source within is beyond Purusha. For them, the eternal existent is Paramashiva, which is the deepest aspect of our own selves. Their form of sadhana helps us expand into all there is because everything is the expression of Paramashiva or the Ultimate Reality, including all disturbances. Disturbances occur within a human being when he is cut off from the Source. When he learns to reconnect the self with the Source, he learns that all is one, and it is not possible to hurt another or oneself.

Buddhism has a very different view of mind. Wedded to the doctrine of 'anitya', impermanence, it rejects all eternal phenomena like Paramshiva, Purusha or atman because it sees everything as impermanent. Impermanence is the fundamental reality in Buddhism.

The purpose of sadhana here is to dissolve not only the ego but also the clinging to atman. This can be achieved by practices meant to steady and sharpen awareness, such as body and breath practices.

Before we look at the different ways yogis have learnt to handle the mind, we should think of a very important verse from the Amritabindu Upanishad:

Mana eva manushyanam karanam bandha mokshyoh
Bandhaya pishyasaktam muktam ye nirvishayam smritam.

(It is the mind that is the cause of bondage
and liberation. The mind that is attached to
sense-objects leads to bondage; the mind that is
dissociated from sense-objects leads to liberation.)

Mind, therefore, is the main arena of both bondage and liberation. Even those who approach spirituality from other doors finally arrive at the threshold of mind. For example, at the culmination of breath or mantra practice, the waves of breath or the sound waves of the mantra are absorbed into the foundation of the deepest mind, which is free from all fluctuations of the ordinary mind. As the seeker, who began with body or breath work, advances in his sadhana, he finds that the physical methods become mental in nature over time. The asanas and pranayamas, in the higher stages of practice, start happening in the mind and the yogi does not need to perform them physically, though the results will affect not just the mind but the body as well.

Now, coming to actual mental practices, meditation is a powerful tool. There are innumerable kinds of meditation that have been taught by great gurus, who evolved them to suit diverse natures. Further, different systems have different kinds of mediation techniques. For example, *Vijnana Bhairava,* a seminal tantric meditation manual, teaches 112 types of meditation. Similarly, Jainism and Buddhism have developed a huge body of meditation practices.

However, meditation can be classified into some basic types based on the school one follows and the intended goal. For ascetic schools like Patanjali yoga, Buddhism, Jainism and Vedanta, the purpose of sadhana is to extricate the self from the machinations of the mind, which occur due to the fascination or repulsion for events and objects of the world. The prerequisite of such meditation is what Patanjali calls 'pratyahara', literally, 'not taking in'. More broadly, it means withdrawal from the fluctuations of the mind or the world.

Pratyahara is a method where one learns not to react to internal or external stimuli. It is suitable for people whose enjoyment of the world has reached a saturation point or those who are temperamentally in favour of detachment. Most well-known yoga schools the world over offer ascetic spiritual solutions to all and sundry, irrespective of their nature or suitability. These are also known as 'exclusivist' schools.

In most cases, this exclusivist approach does more harm than good in the long run. No one can be comfortable with anything that goes against the grain of one's deepest nature for very long. So we need a system that fits our personality type or temperament. Exclusivist schools take the 'neti' approach, which negates everything; inclusivist schools take the 'iti' approach, which divinizes everything.

The practices enjoined by inclusivist schools such as tantra, work for who want to enrich and deepen their love for the world and its pleasures, and to experience the Divine in the world. William Blake writes of this in his 'Auguries of Innocence':

> To see a World in a Grain of Sand
> And a Heaven in a Wild Flower.

The methods employed by these schools help seekers to turn whatever keeps them bound to the world – sex, love of food and drink, a passion for the arts and sciences – into stepping stones for their sadhana. I shall talk more about these desires in later chapters.

Before giving some important examples and providing an account of how this important difference between an inclusive and exclusive approach works out in spiritual practice, we need to understand the basic principle underlying both these approaches. Here lies the need to school and discipline the mind. Shanmukha Swami, a fifteenth-century Kannada saint-poet, puts it well:

> *The monkey of the mind*
> *Has climbed the tree of the body*
> *And, jumping from branch to branch*
> *Of the senses and gathering*
> *Fruits of sensuality,*
> *Is going towards the restless world.*
> *Bind this monkey in the rope*
> *Of your remembrance*
> *And rescue me, O Akhandeshwara.*

In Indian spiritual literature, the mind is often compared to a monkey. Just as a monkey jumps from branch to branch and tree to tree, the mind keeps jumping from thought to thought, image to image. Though this restlessness is basically an expression of the creative energy of the mind, all this jumping around comes to naught because energy is dissipated. The same restless energy needs to be channelled or streamlined for any human achievement.

The popular Indian monkey-god, Hanuman, is a symbol of how the monkey-mind can become a yogi and a powerful god after having disciplined himself through yoga and devotion. Great scientists, artists and socially committed people attain success to the extent they can control the mind and let it focus on the task at hand. This notwithstanding, they cannot alter the overall nature of the mind which, once the task is completed, will start hopping around again.

Since the agitation of the mind is reflected in the agitation of the body and the breath, the practices of asanas and pranayama can be of considerable help in stilling the mind. This is why, whichever type of meditation we want to adopt, we need to first learn to slow down and still the mind. Only then can the mind be ready to take to meditation.

Breathing and body awareness techniques are a very good way to help still the mind. However, the mind is not entirely dependent on the body or the breath. Indian spiritual masters have evolved a whole system of mind-based techniques to calm the mind before meditation can begin. Buddhist mindfulness practices are helpful too.

Breathing and body awareness techniques are equivalent to Patanjali's concept of pratyahara, where you watch inner and outer experiences, observe sensations, feelings and thoughts, without participating in or reacting to them. Without trying to stop the mind forcefully, you just need to watch what is happening to your breath and body.

Similar practices are followed in other schools though the nomenclature changes. In Jainism, such practices are referred to as 'preksha dhyan' or watching meditation. In Vedantic schools, this is called 'antarmouna' or inner silence.

The preliminaries for meditation focus on the aspect of mind called nimesha, which broadly means introversion or focusing inwards. However, the unmesha aspect of mind, that of going out or extroversion, can be tapped to induce inner calm as well. Such methods are part of the bhavana system of meditation, taught in Buddhism and tantra.

Just as body and breath function between the polarities of tension and relaxation, and exhalation and inhalation, the mind also exists between two opposite impulses of extroversion and introversion, expansion and contraction, opening and closing. The extroversion and introversion in the normal mind are not in our control; they do not happen with our free will. But when meditation is perfected, we can contract and expand the mind at will.

These opposite but complimentary tendencies are called unmesha and nimesha in Kashmir Shaivism as well. Together, they constitute spanda, Cosmic

Pulsations, the raison d'être of all processes. In *Spandakarika*, a key text of Kashmir Shaivism, it is written:

Yasyonmesha nimeshabhyam jagatah pralayodayau
Tam Shaktichakra prabhava vivbhavam shankaram
stumah.

(We bow down to Lord Shankara, the driving force
of energy cycles, because of whose opening and
closing of the eyes the cosmos comes into and goes
out of existence.)

In bhavana meditation, instead of stilling the mind into becoming a silent observer, we allow the mind to move but in a particular direction or around a specific imagined experience. Among other things, bhavana means 'being soaked in'; it also means feeling or imagination. Hence the practice of bhavana involves voluntary 'soaking' in a positive experience, albeit imagined. In contemporary parlance, it can be called positive visualization.

Lord Buddha taught several types of bhavana to streamline the mind, the most important of them being metta bhavana, the visualization of the state of compassion; and shanti bhavana, the visualization of the state of peace. In compassion bhavana, for example, one starts by projecting compassion onto oneself by visualizing oneself in a state of optimum satisfaction and abundance. Later, the same kind of visualization is directed to one's family, friends, strangers and even enemies. In this practice, we condemn neither ourselves nor others. We accept and forgive everybody, including our worst enemies. In more advanced meditation, compassion is projected on all sentient beings and even non-living things. My own experience, and that of people close to me, has time and again demonstrated that this is a most powerful practice.

In spiritual schools where deities figure prominently, like in the Indian bhakti traditions or in Tibetan Buddhism, ideal and positive states are embodied as devatas. They are invoked and adored in the heart and mind through the appropriate visual forms and sound forms, which are the mantras of the devatas in question. I have discussed this in the chapter on devatas.

Both the types of practices briefly discussed above – awareness meditations and visualization meditations, are based on the principle that, in spiritual life, instead of treating the mind like it is an enemy to be fought, we treat it as an ally to be won over. This approach is the opposite of that adopted in dualistic schools like Pashupata and other dualistic Shaiva and Vaishnava systems. This is also the approach in belief-dependent faiths, where we enter into a conflict with the mind. Here, defeat is a certainty because we cannot succeed when we declare a never-ending battle with a part of ourselves.

Once we have established a sufficient degree of inner quiet, the usually rebellious mind becomes our close friend. It is now time to start meditation.

In Patanjali's system of yoga, pratyahara, the stilling of the mind, needs to be followed by the next three progressive stages of meditation: dharana (concentration), dhyana (contemplation), and samadhi (absorption). While this is a useful way of describing stages, the unfolding of the meditation does not always happen in this linear fashion. Swami Satyananda said in a satsang in Mumbai in 1984, that meditation is something that happens spontaneously once we have achieved pratyahara – the power to still or move the mind at will.

Bhakti schools hold that the intense love of a god or a goddess in the form of a particular devata can lead to the final state of samadhi without step-by-step processes such as asanas, pranayama and pratayhara. Tantrik schools say that dharana, dhyana and even samadhi can happen through intense shaktipat from a competent guru.

What is the goal we are seeking through the training of the mind? Ascetic schools that emphasize nimesha or withdrawal into the purest essence of the being, suggest the essential goal through words like 'kaivalya', 'nirvana' or 'moksha', meaning freedom from the world. However, according to inclusivist systems like monistic tantra or Mahayana Buddhism, moksha is only half the task; the enlightened being has to return to the world without losing awareness of the Ultimate Reality.

According to the inclusivists, those who attain only samadhi can become slaves of introversion, but those who rise above the blissful state of samadhi and come back to the world, are liberated in the world as they can hold back from, or partake of, the world of becoming, at will and in complete freedom. This state is referred to as jeevanmukti, parashivatva or anuttara.

For systems like monistic tantra and Mahayana Buddhism, mentioned above, the mind and world are experienced as suffering or as a hinderance only so long as we remain benighted by ignorance, the condition of the unenlightened being. Once we succeed in freeing ourselves from the shackles of ignorance through whatever means, we can experience the mind and the world as ananda, limitless bliss.

It is such a vision of absolute joy and perfection that informs one of the greatest statements of the Upanishads:

Om poornamadah poornamidam poornaat
poornamudachyate
Poornasya poornamaadaaya
poornamevaavashishyate.

(Om. This is complete, that is complete
From what is complete comes completeness
When you take completeness from completeness
Only completeness remains.)

Door 7

KAMA

If you can pull out the fang of the serpent
It is good to play with the serpent.

– Akka Mahadevi

KAMA REFERS TO DESIRE IN A VERY BROAD SENSE, AND
includes all kinds of passions. An obvious desire it
refers to is sexual desire, which is the most powerful
kind of yearning.

Kama is an instinct that is very difficult to handle.
Human beings either overindulge in it or run away
from it, because very few people know how to handle
this energy wisely. On the spiritual path, like any other
energy, desire can become either a friend or a foe.

Long before modern psychology discovered the
immense power of sexual desire, Indian spiritual
masters had understood it and had worked out different

ways of managing it. In the traditional Indian world view, kama was one of the four goals of life, the other three being dharma, ethics; artha, wealth; and moksha, salvation. The human life cycle was divided into four ashrams or phases in order to explore and experience these ideals. The first was brahmacharya, when young people were disciplined under the guidance of a guru in the setting of a hermitage. The second was grihasta, where a person got married and lived the life of a householder, pursuing relationships and a livelihood. This phase combined kama and artha. After reaching a certain age of maturity, a person would withdraw from worldly life, first entering vanaprastha, a life in the forest, and then retreating into sanyasa.

To enter into marriage and procreate was part of the adherence to dharma. This was not something limited to princes or merchants but applied to sages as well. Marriage itself was considered sacred because it was part of the journey towards moksha. Sexual desire was an energy to be experienced in the context of a harmonious wordly life.

However, with the rise of ascetic schools of spirituality like Jainism and Buddhism, this attitude to kama changed. While moksha remained the goal, wordly life was considered detrimental to the spiritual path. The goal of the ascetic was to liberate himself from the temptation of the senses. Sex, therefore, was anathema for them. The sexual instinct, along with other worldly pleasures, had to be denied completely. The ascetics encouraged the cultivation of vairagya, non-attachment, because they believed that raga, attachment, could not lead to moksha.

In the *Mahaparinibbana Sutta,* which records the last day of the Buddha's life on this earth, the Blessed One gives his last instructions to his dearest disciple, Ananda. One of them is a strong warning against women. The Buddha enjoins Ananda never to look at women. Ananda asks, 'What if they look at us?' The Lord says, 'Don't talk to them.' Ananda asks again, 'What if they talk to us?' The Buddha says, 'Talk to them while seeing those younger than you as daughters and those older than you as your mothers.' To avoid monks and nuns falling into the 'trap' of lust, Lord Buddha organized the order in such a way that they lived separately. He was apprehensive that, while living in close proximity, monks and nuns might break the vow of brahmacharya.

After Jainism and Buddhism became influential and attracted royal patronage, the fear of kama and the need for brahmacharya passed into other spiritual orders that were competing with them to get political and economic leverage. They rejected the ideals of the sacred relationship between man and woman such as those embodied by Shiva and Parvati, and Radha and Krishna, and imposed on themselves the yoke of brahmacharya.

While the ascetic schools continued this taboo against kama, the tantric schools, on the other hand, adopted a completely contrary view. They wanted to transform this 'block' into a tool for spiritual growth. We have already explored in earlier chapters the fact that sexual union is an essential part of vamachara tantra. In the ritualistic context, man and woman cease to be themselves and become embodiments of the Shiva and Shakti principles central to the yogic world view. The physical union becomes an expression of the cosmic play of Shiva and Shakti.

As I explain in that section, this union is different from ordinary human love because at the height of the union, the participants in the ritual do not allow the emission of sexual fluids. Having trained in techniques of hatha yoga, tantrics know how to pull back into themselves that sexual energy and direct it to the crown chakra, thereby transforming sexual energy into divine energy. While ordinary people use sex in a way that keeps them tied to the materialistic world, tantric yogis use the same power as a means of release from conditioned existence.

As I have also shared, practitioners of dakshinachara tantra bring about the union of Shiva and Shakti within the body, without the need of a sexual partner. Thus vamachara and dakshinachara sadhana arrive at the same goal: the joyous union of Shiva and Shakti, but through different means.

The bhakti schools, on the other hand, emphasize the emotional aspect of love instead of manifesting it in physical terms. The desire involved in human love is sublimated into love for the Divine. Bhakti schools talk about different bhavas, emotions, to approach the Divine. These include sakhya, friendship; dasa, love as servitude; vatsalya, the love of the child for the parent; vaira, hatred; and madhurya, the sweetness of sexual love.

All these forms of love are projected onto the deity instead of a human being. For example, the spontaneous feeling of sexual love, which is normally directed to a human figure, is projected instead onto a divine form imagined to be far more beautiful and powerful than the human beloved. In fact, it can also happen that human love is experienced and found inadequate. Women bhaktas like Andal, Kaaraikkaal Ammai of Tamil Nadu, Akka Mahadevi of Karnataka and Lalleshawari of Kashmir found bliss in divine love only after they walked out of their marriages.

Bhakti is basically the way of the heart. It employs the imagination to the point where what is imagined becomes more real than objective reality. But this cannot be interpreted as delusion, because the delusional self is unaware of the inner self. The practitioner of bhakti uses the imagination consciously and purposively, like an artist does, to connect with the Divine.

There is another possibility that exists in the bhakti tradition, although this is often ignored by the spiritual traditions. Here, human love is not replaced by divine love; instead, human love is experienced as an extension of divine love. Every action becomes an act of worship, and this includes the love between a husband and wife. Through the ages, a lot of bhakta couples have lived harmonious family lives during their bhakti sadhana, and they have not been celibate.

The twelfth-century vachana poet, Dasimayya the weaver, writes that 'the devotion in which the man and the woman unite is pleasing to Shiva; the devotion in which man and woman do not unite is like mixing nectar with poison.' Tamil Shaivite saint Sundarar's polygamous love for women was no obstacle to his devotion to Shiva. Even Shiva had no objection to it. The Divine can become an aid and ally in the devotee's pursuit of amorous adventures.

The life and work of the famous Sanskrit poet Jayadeva also shows that there is no contradiction between human love and divine love. Jayadeva was a lover and a bhakta at the same time; he worshipped Hari and adored Padmavati. One of the greatest literary works in the bhakti traditions, his *Gita Govinda*, addresses both devotees of Lord Hari as well as those interested in love and sexuality. In the poem, Lord Krishna is repeatedly disloyal to his beloved Radha, who is the epitome of constancy. But at the end of the poem, Krishna owns up to his failings and surrenders to Radha's love.

What needs to be underlined is the complementarity, not the opposition, between physical and spiritual love, both in the bhakti traditions and in tantra, in spite of the assertion sometimes to the contrary.

To know how powerful the sexual urge is, one only needs to look at stories from Indian mythology. Kama, the god of love, is irresistibly handsome. Associated with spring, he is visualized as being armed with a sugarcane bow and arrows made up of flowers. His wife, Rati, is known for her beauty. Though they are benevolent to people who are in love, they strike terror in the hearts of ascetics. Kama is endowed with great power, and is the son of Lord Vishnu.

In myths and legends, gods and yogis repeatedly came into conflict with Kama. Even Lord Shiva with his unparalleled powers could only win a temporary victory over him. Once, the gods needed Shiva to come out of his samadhi because only a son begotten by him could defeat the demon, Taraka, who had subdued all the gods. When, at their behest, Kama disturbed Lord Shiva absorbed in deep meditation, the infuriated Shiva opened his third eye and sent flames Kama's way, reducing him to ashes. Parvati had to cast her healing glance at Kama to bring him back to life. Exactly at this moment, Shiva's gaze fell on Parvati, and Kama took this opportunity to enter Shiva's body, thereby transforming the ascetic god into Kameshwara, the lord of love and desire. Thus, Shiva, who was called Kamari, the foe of desire, became Kameshwara, eternally conjoined to his beloved Parvati.

The wisest and most skilled of Indian poets, Kalidasa, made this the theme of his great poem 'Kumarasambhava'. Among other things, this poem was a corrective to ascetic faiths that had begun to uphold celibacy as the highest virtue. Though Patanjali included celibacy as a virtue to be practised before one ventured into the succeeding stages of yoga, the love of man and woman began to figure prominently in tantric and bhakti cultures.

However, the history and mythology of spirituality demonstrate that the more people try to exile the god of love, the more determindly he comes back in you in some form or another. When the sage Vishvamitra developed immense powers as a result of his sadhana, Indra was worried. The king sent Menaka to tempt the sage and as you know, Vishwamitra yielded to the apsara's charms and broke his vow of celibacy. Kama's power was much stronger than the power the sage had accumulated through many years of austerities. The problem was that Vishwamitra had not come to terms with the sexual urge in him, assuming he was free of it.

So, how does one deal with one's sexuality on the spiritual path? There are several ways, as I have made clear. The avoidance of sex is only one way, but it is not without its problems, and celibacy has to be approached with awareness. Sex is not a door that necessarily shuts us to a spiritual life; it can also be a legitimate door that leads us in. In one way or another, the sexual urge has to be acknowledged and accepted before it can be transformed or transcended.

Door 8

KARMA AND KAYAKA

THE WORDS 'KARMA' AND 'KAYAKA' BOTH REFER TO what we do. Karma refers to a very broad spectrum of actions while kayaka refers specifically to labour performed for livelihood.

The creative urge is innate in human beings, and manifests in different ways. Apart from procreating and perpetuating the species, mankind has performed physical and mental labour to create cultures and build up civilizations through human history.

Both karma and kayaka provide alternatives to ascetic modes of spirituality, which advocate a withdrawal from the world of actions. However, the performance of karma, actions, and kayaka, labour, done with attention and awareness, can become a doorway that takes us to spiritual realization. When actions are done with awareness, they become a form of dynamic meditation.

On the other hand, if they are done unconsciously, under duress or with an eye only on the profits they bring, then they become a block on the spiritual path.

Hence, karma and kayaka are other tools that the modern spiritual seeker can use for spiritual growth while living in the world.

Karma is a recurring word in different spiritual schools of India. It has several shades of meaning but all of them are related to deeds, doing, actions, activity and professional work.

In Buddhism and Jainism, as also in Vedic and tantric traditions, 'karma' has a special meaning: it is the result of past actions, good or bad, which we experience now and in the future. This meaning assumes greater significance in Buddhism and Jainism, the two atheistic faiths, where liberation from bondage is possible only through one's own actions and not on the grace of any higher force. In theistic traditions such as the Vedic and tantric ones, this meaning is relevant but there is also scope for alleviating the effect of bad deeds of the past through anugraha, the grace of a higher being such as the guru, deity, or the Divine.

Karma also has a positive side to it. It is not just the philosophy of predeterminism; it is also the philosophy that promises freedom because we can alter the effects of the past by good deeds in the present. It involves making the decision to change the results of the past by corrective actions in the present. A person who has fallen sick due to unhealthy habits in the past can correct this by following a healthy lifestyle and taking the appropriate medical remedies.

When we extend the meaning of karma to the sum total of an individual's actions that predetermine his life patterns, karma becomes a law of moral equilibrium in the world. One gets good or bad results for his efforts depending on the sum total of his actions in the past. If one believes in reincarnation, which many Indian spiritual schools do, the consequences of karma follow one in future incarnations as well. Before Siddhartha Gautama attained enlightenment in his last life, he had performed good karmas as a bodhisattva in many past lives. Due to this, he was able to attain enlightenment in his final life.

Before Jain Tirthankaras attain kaivalya, pure knowledge, in their final incarnation, they have to pass through many lives on different planes in the cosmos, exhausting their craving for enjoyment. When the time arrives, they take birth on the human plane to experience disillusionment with the lure of the senses and then take to the Jain path of ascetism and austerity. To attain liberation from samsara, they have to perform pious karmas in the present life.

Karma is not just limited to individuals; collectives such as countries and communities have their own karmas too. If a certain kind of tyranny visits a community or a nation, this is the sum total of their collective actions in the past. Our karma is influenced not only by our own actions but also by other people's actions. Despite driving carefully, we may meet with an accident when another person is driving irresponsibly. During times of collective disasters, some people with strong positive individual karmas – the result of past deeds – can escape the mayhem.

Even if we forget the belief in reincarnation and take a balanced view of our mundane experiences, we see how our actions brings about certain kinds of results. As you sow, so shall you reap: this is a lesson of everyday experience.

When ascetic faiths like Buddhism and Jainism became popular in ancient India, there was a rush among the common people to enter their fold and become monks, abandoning their jobs and families. These faiths focused on a withdrawal from the world, practicing austerities to free oneself from the cycle of karma. It is in this context that the Bhagavad Gita introduces the philosophy of karma yoga as taught by Lord Krishna to Arjuna.

In the context of karma yoga, karma also refers to professions in society. Both the Buddha and Lord Krishna also use karma in this sense. The Buddha's recipe for the noble eight-fold path, leading to the end of sorrow, includes 'sammakammanta', the right profession. Lord Krishna goes further and equates karma with yoga when he says 'yoga karmasukaushalam', skillful karma is yoga. If you perform your professional duties with care, this is also yoga.

This teaching was imparted by Lord Krishna to Arjuna when the latter was confronted with his existentialist crisis on the battlefield. On the eve of the battle, Arjuna felt despondent as he was about to fight a war with his gurus and kinsmen. He was tempted to opt out of this unenviable situation by abandoning the battle he knew would result in bloodshed and mayhem. But Lord Krishna persuaded him against this renunciation.

Lord Krishna taught Arjuna that the practice and philosophy of karma yoga requires that performing one's socially-entrusted duty with detachment and equanimity is yoga, and a means of achieving freedom from karmic bondage. This philosophy is paraphrased in the following verse in the Bhagavad Gita:

Karmanye vadhikaaraste ma phaleshu kada cha na
Ma karma phalaheturbhurmateysangostava
akarmani.

(You have the right only to perform your action, but not to its fruits. Do not work thinking of the fruits or become attached to inaction.)

Lord Krishna teaches that the path of action, when accompanied by detachment from its results, is a complete approach to spirituality. This means that just performing the labour assigned to you, but with complete devotion and awareness, and indifference to the fruits of action, can lead you to salvation. He further points out that, in spite of being the greatest of gods, he himself is not exempt from performing his cosmic duties. What the Lord of the Universe practises at the cosmic level to preserve cosmic order, Arjuna is told to perform in society to preserve the social order. Being born into the warrior caste of Kshatriyas, he is duty-bound to fight. Only if he renounces attachment to the result of his action, can he attain the same liberation that others attain through different means like devotion or meditation.

While preaching karma yoga, the social order that the Bhagavad Gita upheld was one based on caste hierarchy, where each caste had specific duties to perform. While the lower caste had to work very hard, the Brahmins and the orders of monks of different sects began to enjoy the bountiful patronage of kings whose sacred duty was to offer daan, generous gifts of land and wealth, to them. Neither the givers nor takers of daan obtained wealth or lands through their own labour. Kings accumulated their wealth by looting enemies during war and the common people during peacetime. In the context of such an exploitive order, karma yoga, enjoining the performance of caste duties, could become a means of promoting the greed of the privileged.

The kind of 'subsidized' lives the priests and monks lived violated a moral injunction that is imperative in many spiritual traditions. Patanjali had imposed the rule of aparigraha, non-possessiveness. The Buddhist code for monks prescribed that they possess nothing beyond bare necessities like a begging bowl, a staff and two pieces of saffron clothes to cover themselves. Jain monks give up even the basic necessities. As contrasted with this ideal, the reality of rich orders of monks, which are rife even now, was ridiculed by the twentieth-century Kannada poet Gopalakrishna Adiga in a poem of his:

The pose of sitting firmly on poisoned
Wealth, gold, possessions, carriages
Seals of gold-coated pure brass
Good not for this world or the next.

The most consistent critique of this institution of daan came from the sharanas, artisan saints who lived in Karnataka during the twelfth century and practised Shaivite bhakti. Their ethical code proscribed the acceptance of wealth and women 'belonging' to somebody else. This vow is illustrated in a daring poem by Satyakka, a woman saint of this period. This is what she has to tell Lord Shiva:

I promise you
That I will never stretch my hand
To seek alms of bribes or favours
Even when I see gold or some precious thing
Fallen on the road.
I will not take it
I will not even touch it, I swear
In the name of your holy servants
Because I live by the alms you give me
If I am ever drawn to another's wealth
Drown me in perdition
And leave me for ever
O Lord Shabhujakkeshwara.

This obviously referred to the ill-gotten wealth of rulers, a portion of which was conferred on the priestly and monastic classes. The sharanas opposed the system of daan with that of dasoha, which is the offering the seeker makes to holy mendicants who accept offerings only from devotees, not from kings.

The sharanas essentially replaced the notion of karma yoga with the yoga of kayaka, manual labour, which was performed not as a result of caste duty but as a means of livelihood, carried out with concentration and mindfulness like worship or meditation. The spiritual practice of the artisans of the sharana community was an alternative to the devotional path involving absorption in God and turning away from daily life.

The sharanas describe kayaka yoga in their fiery spiritual poems called vachanas. The kayaka yoga depicted in these poems provides a paradigm of a spiritual path to all of us no matter what kind of labour we pursue for our livelihood. It also obviates the need for other forms of yoga.

Dasimayya the weaver describes how his profession of weaving becomes the means of attaining spiritual heights.

After tightening the wrap
After arranging the golden border
After pushing the peddle down
With feet so that the frame
Moves up and down
The shuttle's point
Eats up the skein
Who weaves this saree
You or me
O Ramanatha?

Channayya the cobbler elevates the act of making a pair of sandals into a spiritual experience:

After erecting three pillars
The gross, the subtle and the casual bodies

After beating the buffaloes' rough hide
After removing the flesh
With the staff of the manifest and the hidden
After tanning the hide with the fibre of dualism
After pouring the caustic juice of quintessence
Into the hide pouch of awareness
The blemishes of the soul thus destroyed
I have come
To take the sandals to his feet
Take care
Not of the ground below
But of the path your feet and sandals take
Do not be enslaved
By the hand-awl, blade or peg
But realize
Ramarama, your own true self, joy of joys.

Even Maritande, a burgler by profession, has no qualms
about experiencing the spiritual dimension of his trade
that may appear contemptible to other people:

For my picklock master
I slaughtered a goat
Sacrificed a monkey
Gave away my parents
If, in spite of all this,
The stolen object does not come

To me lovingly
I declare:
Lord of Mara, the love god
The foe of haste
Does not exist.

If I am a thief at night
That would be a shame
To the master
Who gave me the picklock
If I enter the houses
When people are forgetful
That would be a shame
To my art
I wake up the forgetful
Show them their riches
And then
Bring out my own too
O Father
Lord of Mara, the love god
The foe of haste.

Ramanna the cowherd saint-poet, perceives the cycles of cosmic time in his daily labour:

I keep vigil of Rudra
At night

After I drive the herd
Back to their folds
O when shall I be rid
Of this cowherd's staff
No, the cowherd's staff
Shall not drop
From my hands
Until Vishweshwaralinga
The lord of cowherds
Ceases to be.

Another saint poet, Chowdayya the ferryman, sees mirrored in his everyday labour the whole spiritual journey:

Here I come, a bodiless ferryman
To the great river
If you pay the price, your mind
That grasps and lets go
I will take you across
The great stream
To the last village
Without words or limits
Says Chowdayya the ferryman.

Play-acting on the part of street performers may reflect a journey from form to that which is formless:

Entering from behind a nondescript curtain
Putting on many guises
Of the lord of all beasts
I shattered the amplifier
Tore up the curtain
Proclaiming
Living beings do not exist
I was hailing Naginatha, dear to Rekanna.

When a conflict arises between devotion to labour and devotion to the deity, these artisan saints prefer to choose labour instead of the deity. This is the point that Dhoolalayya, another cobbler saint-poet makes in the following poem:

On seeing the great Lord
Appear on the edge of the chisel
Piercing the hide
'Why are you here, Sir
In front of the one that moves about
Carrying the bag of flesh?
Go away
To the dwelling place of your devotees
Free them
Go on the top of your silver mountain,
With your masquerades
Go, free your devotees.

By the grace of the Master of Lust,
Dust and Smoke
Go and prosper.'

As if speaking for all artisan and labouring saint-poets for whom manual labour, apart from being a means of livelihood, is also a way of life leading to ultimate freedom here and now, says Chandayya the ropemaker:

Labour alone frees the guru from life
Labour alone frees linga
From its kinship with stone
Labour alone frees the jangama
From his outer appearance
Listen Prabhu
This is the teaching
Of Chandeshwaralinga.

Door 9

PRATIBHA

THE SANSKRIT WORD 'PRATIBHA' REFERS TO THE creative light within, which radiates outwards through creative expressions. Like its English equivalent 'imagination', it refers to the ability to create. Pratibha is central to the theory of arts and poetics in Sanskrit. Both 'pratibha' and 'imagination' suggest mirroring or reflecting; imagination also means imaging or reflecting.

In Western thought, at least two great poets, William Blake and Coleridge, tried to elevate the aesthetic concept of imagination to the spiritual plane. For Blake, it was not just the faculty that expresses itself in art or poetry but also connotes the vision of the prophets who can look beyond the limitations of time and place. He therefore called it 'Jesus the Imagination'. Coleridge, in his *Biographia Literia*, defined 'Imagination', as a higher poetic faculty than fancy, as 'the repetition in the finite mind of the eternal I AM'. But for such exceptions, the Western concept of imagination is an aesthetic and not a spiritual category.

Pratibha has a close connection with the spiritual realm, particularly in Kashmir Shaiva philosophy. As an aesthetic impulse, it is what enables poets to create poetry. Acharya Abhinavagupta, a great yogi and aesthetician who lived in Kashmir in the tenth century, defined pratibha as 'apoorva vastu nirmana kshama prajna' (the wisdom capable of producing things with no precedent). This definition underscores the point that art is not an imitation of nature or something external. Instead, it is an unfolding from within. Kashmir Shaivite metaphysics views the cosmos as the creative expression of the Cosmic Lord, who is also the Cosmic Poet. This unfolding happens without the help of anything external, as depicted in a hymn to Sri Dakshinamurti (the cosmic form of Shiva as Guru), ascribed to Shankaracharya:

Bijasayantarivaankuro jagadidam punar
prannirvikalpam tatha
Mayaakalpita desha kaala kalana
vaichitrachitreekeutam
Mayaaviiva vijrubhayate mahayogi iva yah
swechchaya.

(This whole cosmos is contained in the Primal Consciousness, like in a seed. Like a great yogi shining forth, it creates out of its own will maya, which imagines space, time and movement.)

Most spiritual gurus interpret the word 'maya' as illusion. However, the majority of traditional Indian schools of philosophy do not ascribe this meaning to maya. For example, in the tantric schools of Shaivism and Shaktism, maya is understood as the creative power of the cosmic consciousness. The ability of the Cosmic Lord to create the cosmos with the help of this power called maya is cosmic pratibha.

In other words, cosmic pratibha is the poetic faculty of the cosmos to create, just as the individual poet uses pratibha for his individual poetic expression. As I mentioned, the cosmos is the poem of the Cosmic Lord, and he creates this through the faculty of pratibha or imagination, while the magical principle and process through which he creates is called maya.

Pratibha is often personified as Pratibhadevi, the goddess of imagination. However, the pratibha of a poet, though similar to the cosmic pratibha of Paramashiva in that both are the unfolding of swantantrya shakti, creative freedom, are not identical. This is because the Cosmic Poet, Paramashiva, is free from the human limitations of time, space and change.

The human poet expresses his freedom within the spectrum of time and space. Only when fully enlightened, can human beings understand that they are none other than Paramashiva. However, on the limited human plane, they can have a foretaste of the unfettered bliss of Paramashiva. So, the experience of art is similar to but not identical with the spiritual experience of enlightenment. Vishvanatha, the author of *Sahitya Darpana*, describes the creative process as 'brahmanadasodara', the younger brother of enlightenment.

The schools of Indian spirituality such as tantra and bhakti recognize the continuum between pratibha and spirituality. These schools also use poetry, music, sculpture and painting for spiritual practice and expression, for they do not negate but celebrate the world of the senses.

Meanwhile, ascetic spiritual paths like Pali Buddhism and Jainism see the sensory and sensual world as a trap. They focus on denying pleasure because they perceive the *world* to be the site of misery and bondage. According to them, it is the attachment to the pleasures of the world that keeps one tied to this fundamentally painful reality. These pleasures, they believe, are transient and lead eventually to sorrow. Dispassion and restraint will bring not only freedom from sorrow but also a higher kind of pleasure and peace, which will endure.

This is why ascetic schools see art as an illusion that tempts one away from spirituality. Time and again, Lord Buddha tells his disciples that the nature of nibbana, spiritual liberation, is one of unadulterated bliss. To attain this goal, one has to cut off all pleasures, including the delight that we experience in creating and savouring works of art. The strict methods followed by those on ascetic paths help them develop a distaste for the things they once enjoyed.

In the seminal Pali text, *Mahaparinibbana Suttam*, Lord Buddha's final instructions to his monks are recorded. As he lies on his death bed, he is asked by Ananda to share with him how he became enlightened. One of the main reasons that the Buddha cites as the cause of his enlightenment is his rejection of the ensnaring prattle of poetry and art. It is because of this belief that the monks of the order are prohibited from indulging in things that arouse sensual desires: incense, dance, drama, music and, of course, women.

Nevertheless, after Lord Buddha's passing away, the local kings of Kushinara organized a two-week-long celebration to pay their respects to the Blessed One. The celebration included a full-fledged play on the life and sacred deeds of Lord Buddha. Thus, the life of the great master who kept away from the arts came to be celebrated through them. In later periods, Buddhism inspired great works of sculpture and architecture in

India and other parts of the world. After Buddhism split into Hinayana and Mahayana, the latter school was influenced by tantra and actually started using art as a means of spiritual practice.

Thus, the ascetic paths see creative expressions as delusions. Nevertheless, artistic creations have been expressions of spirituality through the ages even in world-negating schools, which is a contradiction of their tenets. Therefore, the pursuit of art, music, dance, poetry and other creative works is definitely a doorway to inner illumination, not only in world-affirming schools but also in world-negating ones.

As we can see, there are two contrary approaches to spiritual life though the goal is the same – to eliminate suffering and attain bliss. One way is to shun or restrain the senses and desires; the other is to transform those very desires into a means of spiritual growth. Those wedded to the first approach distance themselves from the imagination and its expressions; those in the second group embrace art and imagination and make them companions on the spiritual path.

Central to Buddhism are awareness-based meditations outlined in *Satipathana Suttam*, a manual of Buddhist meditation techniques as taught by the Buddha himself. The purpose of Buddhist meditation is to realize the non-existence of any principle of continuity. When we apply awareness to anything within or outside us, we ultimately realize, first-hand, the truth of impermanence. The continuous flow of experience breaks into discrete units where no continuity is perceptible. Long periods of meditation bring us equilibrium, resulting in the cessation of raga, clinging, and its opposite, dosa, hatred, these being the two sources of attachment to conditioned existence.

The Buddhist path is of immense help to those who are either temperamentally against the pleasures of life or have become saturated with the pleasures of worldly life. It trains them to give up the world and find peace in monkhood. However, as I have explained it does not suit people who are artistically inclined because art is inspired by desires and produces things of beauty, which are a joy forever.

I have come to this conclusion on the testimony of my own experience of such practices and of people close to me. My dear departed friend K.M. Shankarappa was a brilliant filmmaker. A student of the great Bengali filmmaker Ritwik Ghatak, he was widely read and was preparing for a very promising film career. But he started taking a very deep interest in philosophy and the practice of Buddhism. A few years later, he lost all interest in cinema. His refrain was: 'It is all dukkha.' His income began to dwindle and then completely disappeared. He bore it all with superhuman patience and without trying to repair the situation. When he passed away, the world lost a magnificent artist who had wasted his enormous talents.

I have also seen a brilliant and prosperous relative of his to whom a similar thing happened. This person was an enterprising engineer who went to Japan and set up his own company, which brought him rich dividends. During this phase, he became a Buddhist and started practicing meditation intensely. He lost all interest in his business and his fortune ebbed away. Returning to India with very little money, he set up a small mechanic shop in Bangalore. When I met him, he said nothing except for the fact that meditation made sense to him. He was content with his meager income and his modest life. Ambition and affluence, he had come to see, can never lead to peace of mind.

Let me share with you my own experience of Buddhist meditation for over three years under the guidance of a powerful meditation teacher, Acharya Buddha Rakkhita Thera, in Bangalore during the eighties. As I progressed in meditation, my wild and agitated mind became calm and patient, and this was a wonderful thing to happen. In the meantime, I began to lose my taste for anything beautiful in life. The food I ate felt tasteless; the music I heard sounded like noise; sex was frightening. And, worst of all, my ability to compose poetry started disappearing. When this fear gripped me, I spoke to my master. He said: 'Let it go, my dear. Tell yourself it is all dukkha.' He was referring to letting go of my pleasures as well as my creative abilities. He was impressed by my commitment and progress, and was getting ready to send me to a meditation centre in Burma.

However, I had to walk out of this situation. For me, life was nothing without poetry. How could I give up poetry, being someone whose interest in spirituality was whetted by the wonderful spiritual poetry of my language? I had the greatest respect for Buddhist practices, but it was not for the likes of me. If this realization had not dawned on me, my life would be very different.

I am not for a moment belittling the great tradition of Buddhist meditation, and it is ideal for those aspiring to live a life away from wordly pleasures and creative pursuits. But I understood it was not right for me. I was also aware that there were other schools of Buddhism like Tibetan Vajrayana and Japanese Zen, whose methods did not lead to a distaste for the world and its beauty. Having no access to them though, I took to the practices of kriya yoga and mantra yoga of the Shaiva and Shakta schools, which refine one's taste for the arts, beauty and the world.

Before I proceed to give an account of how non-ascetic schools of tantra and bhakti employ pratibha and its expressions, I need to describe two aspects of pratibha. This is an important distinction made by Rajashekhara, a scholar of the Shaivite tantra of Kashmir and an authority on poetics. According to him, pratibha, which enables poets to create poetry, is also the faculty that enables connoisseurs to taste the delights of poetry. The poets' pratibha is 'karayatri pratibha', creative imagination; the pratibha of the one who is experiencing poetry is 'bhavayatri pratibha', receptive imagination. Both these faculties are essential for artistic communication and are employed in the spiritual practices of non-ascetic schools. The creative and receptive sides of imagination are like the two wings of the same door.

Visualization is an integral part of sadhana in bhakti yoga and tantra. The statues of temples and paintings of different kinds are manifestations of the way the deity is glimpsed by the worshipper or practitioner. The particular form of the deity is imagined and meditated on before chanting or singing. This enables the heart of the practitioner to participate intimately in worship, whether it is inner or external worship. In inner worship or in meditation upon the deity, the form of the deity is held in the temple of the heart or in the third eye chakra.

The magnificent temples of India have some of the greatest sculptures in the country, depicting the beauty of gods and goddesses. For example, the images of Nataraja in Chidambaram and the sleeping Vishnu in

Sreerangam in Tamil Nadu are exquisite works of art as well as deities for spiritual contemplation.

Great bhaktas carve the form of their beloved deity in words, through poetic and prose compositions. This is how Kalidasa visualizes the goddess Shyamala in *Shyamala Dandakam*:

Chaturbhuje chandrakalavatamse
Kuchonnate kunkumaragashone
Pundrekshu pashankusha pushpa baana haste
Namaste Namaste jagadeka matah.

(The sole mother of the Universe
Four-armed, decked with the digit of the moon
Huge-bosomed, glowing in vermillion red
Holding a sugarcane bow, flower shafts
The noose and the hook
I bow down to her.)

Bhaktas go to the extent of declaring that the joy that yogis attain in samadhi, they can experience when they feast their eyes on the deity's enchanting form. Says Purandara Dasa:

Kangalidyaatako kaveri rangana kanade
Jagangalolage mangala muruti
Rangana sripadangala kanade.

(What is the point in having eyes
Unless you have seen Ranga, the lord on the banks
of Kaveri
Unless you see the most auspicious form
In all the worlds?)

Songs and music are the most frequent expressions of bhakti. Saint poets attain bliss by composing them and devotees feel the same bliss listening to them. Bhakti poetry and music, a precious Indian heritage, is still being savoured all over the country.

Yogis speak of two kinds of music: one that is ahad, outer, and the other that is anahad, inner. Bhakti practices worship through music that is heard. Tantrik sadhana, on the other hand, explores the inner and unheard music in nadayoga, music yoga. Yogic philosophy believes that music without is a grosser form of the subtle inner music audible to the inner ear in deep states of concentration. Listening attentively to this internal music is the path to liberation in nadayoga. Kabir says:

Sunta hai guru jyani
Jeeni jeeni jeeni
Gagan me avaaz ho rahi
Jheeni jheeni jheeni
Oham soham-baja baje
Trikuti dham suhani re

Ida pingala sukhman naari
Sunat bhajan pahrani ho ji
Kahat kabira suno bhai saadho
Jaani agam ke baani re
Din bhar re jo nazar bhar dekhe
Ajar amar nishani re.

(He listens, the wise disciple of the guru
the voice heard in the inner sky,
How beautiful is the music is playing in the
eyebrow centre!
Pleasing to the two women, ida and pingala
Who are pleased with the hymn
'Listen, brothers', says Kabir:
'I have understood meaning of the scriptures
Fill your eyes the whole day
With the vision of the immortal.')

Apart from music, the devotional traditions have nurtured other creative expressions such as dance and theatre. For example, Kathak in north India and Kuchipudi in the south were originally shaped by the bhakti traditions, and so were the immensely popular forms of theatre like the Ramlila, Kathakali, Krishna Attam and Bayalata, to name a few. The services offered in traditional temples included devotional music, dance and theatre.

The pratibha of bhakti expresses itself most in the verbal arts. There is a massive body of spontaneous and passionate outbursts and story-telling of many varieties in all regional languages in India. Since the songs composed by bhakti poets were meant for singing and dancing, and their stories for acting, they could reach not just the learned but the illiterate multitudes.

The most vibrant expression of devotional and tantric pratibha in Indian art and mythology is the image of the dancing Shiva, Nataraja, who is celebrated in sculpture, painting and poetry by bhaktas, and contemplated by yogis and tantriks in their meditation. His dance embodies the ecstasy of the cosmos where all is rhythm and music. See how Rabindranath Tagore celebrates Nataraja:

While dancing the dance of pralaya
Forgetting yourself, O Nataraja
Your matted locks were spread out loose
The Ganga too unleashed her flood

As if mad, she lost the sense of direction
Her waves and ripples rose up to notes of music
When the sun responded to the horizon
Promising fearlessness to all the homeless
Following the flow, she turned her own companion
Whoever had lost all, found all on her banks.

This is how Tagore's poetic pratibha captures the dancing pratibha of Paramashiva, Universal Concsiousness. Paramshiva has two aspects: movement and stillness. The dancing Shiva represents movement; the meditating Shiva represents stillness, which is the peace and stillness that the ascetic faiths seek. This state is also represented in sculpture and poetry in the images of Shiva, the Buddha and Mahavira absorbed in deep contemplation, as well as in the symbolism of the shivalingam. Here is a hymn to Shiva's stillness, composed by the famous Bengali playwright, Girish Chandra Ghosh:

Jogasane mahadhyane magono jogibor
Ananta tushare jeno ananta shekhor
Shishu shashi nahi ar andhokaar niraakaar
Eko nahi dui nahi prakruti nithoro.

(The greatest of yogis is sitting in deep meditation
In his yogic pose.
All around, snow spreads endlessly when he is
In self-absorption.
Not even the crescent moon is visible
In the immense formless dark.
There is no one or two anywhere
When nature is all stillness.)

Such are the instances of how pratibha creates and savours the spiritual forms and landscapes in art and poetry, and becomes an important door to the inner realm, which all of us can enter. In the recipient, the doors of pratibha, as receptive imagination, open when our hearts open.

Yet, art philosophers like Abhinavagupta refused to equate the art experience with the ultimate spiritual experience. They extolled art as an aesthetic joy that gives only a foretaste of the spiritual experience. However, another great expert of poetics, Bhattanayaka, went to the extent of placing the poetic experience way *above* the spiritual experience:

The joy that the goddess of poetry gives to the recipient due to her love for him is greater than the joy that the yogis talk about.

Door 10

ANUTTARA

THE FINAL DOOR IS ANUTTARA, WHICH MEANS THE unsurpassed state. Literally, it means that beyond which there is nothing. This is the door of doors, where all doors open, and where all doors close.

Paradoxically, this last door is also the first one. This is because the spiritual experience of unfettered freedom happens not in time but beyond the space–time continuum, in a realm where everything is present.

Due to the habit of language and memory, our everyday mind imposes meaning and space-time linearity on concepts and objects. We become completely disoriented when the sequence is broken, as linearity is the only order that the intellect is comfortable with. Under conditions of extreme joy or agony, however, linearity breaks down as it does in heightened states of spiritual experience. Only the 'here and now' remains.

The state of 'here and now' is hard to describe, though this is the goal of the spiritual journey. So long as we live in linear time, we live in bondage and becoming. This is the dimension that Buddhists refer to as impermanence and misery. In other schools, it is called bhava, endless becoming. By contrast, in the state of liberation, then and now, here and there – the pillars of ego consciousness, fall away. Negatively defined, this state is called nibbana, stripping away; in positive terms, it is called moksha, freedom. However, a more comprehensive term for the state or consciousness of liberation is anuttara. Another way to describe it is to say that it is the experience of timelessness in time.

Anuttara can be seen in another way as well. In this state, being and becoming, constancy and change, 'I' and the 'Cosmos' are simultaneously present. Shaivism calls this state 'poornahanta', the totality of the Self, which is the nature of Paramashiva. The sharana philosophers of Karnataka call the same state 'nishunya', non-emptiness. It is not the end of the journey, but the end of all ends and beginnings. One is uprooted from the flow of time and from spatial coordinates: here and there; above and below. Allama Prabhu describes this state in the following poem:

Look!
The infinity of the past and the infinity of the future
Were contained in a single day
Who can spot the ultimate being
Who speaks after containing that single day?
Because the ancients, the wise ones, the
innumerable great ones
Could not understand Linga, the infinite one,
They lost their way, O Goggeshwara.

In our lives, within the spectrum of time and space, we are usually busy trying to get somewhere to attain peace and contentment. When we do get somewhere, we feel that we should have reached another point, and this is how roads lead on endlessly. This kind of aimless wandering and restlessness leads to frustration, the state of endless becoming mentioned above.

Then, we seek refuge from the fatigue and restlessness of the journey we are on. We take holidays; we go on pilgrimages and adventure trips. But all escapes have their beginnings and ends. When we return, we are back where we started, back in the cycle of our aimless wandering, longing for the next holiday so we can 'recharge' ourselves. We try and escape the emptiness within in countless ways: there are parties and addictions and love affairs and a thousand other preoccupations that keep us trapped.

The more intellectually inclined among us try to find solace in books and philosophies. A life of the mind and intellect, and engagements in the arts and creative expressions undoubtedly help us break out of the annoyance and fatigue of everyday life for considerable periods of time. But here too, eventually, questions lead to other questions and explanations to other explanations. We are back again in the same cycle of quest after quest.

When, finally, we realize that these pursuits of pleasure are getting us nowhere, we start shopping around in the spiritual world. What we tried to find elsewhere, we now try to find in spiritual life through courses, workshops, retreats and so on.

Yet, after the initial excitement and relief, we start getting bored in this pursuit as well. In fact, most of the gurus we turn to have themselves nowhere to turn. It is like the blind leading the blind.

All of us are like the Sufi humorist Mullah Nasruddin. Mullah once lost his keys. He went out to the city center looking desperately for them. He searched the entire day but couldn't find them. He started beating his chest, weeping and wailing to the passersby: 'Please, somebody help me get my keys.' The more sympathetic folks felt pity for him, and began to walk up and down the area to find the keys. At last, an intelligent young man asked Mullah: 'Are you sure that this is where you lost your keys?' Mullah said, 'No. I lost them last night in a dark room in my house.' The people who had gathered around burst into laughter. Mullah explained, 'It's true; I lost it in the dark room. I can't look for them there because there is no light. I am looking for them here because there is so much light.'

The dark room in the parable stands for the blocked regions within ourselves, places where our deepest wounds and traumas are hidden. Until we have the courage to enter this room we have locked up and forgotten about, we will repeat the cycles of temporary excitements and frustrations. Mullah at least knew where the keys were, but we don't. A great Sufi master, he was playing this drama to remind us of our own stupidity of looking for solutions where they are never to be found. Unless we find that locked room, unlock it and enter it, we are doomed to wander endlessly. Unless spiritual practices lead to this recognition – that the truth, light and joy we seek are within us, they are meaningless. Only when we live this recognition can we enter the state of anuttara.

I have shown you several doors through this book, and each can take us to the state of anuttara. But the only path that can truly take us there is the path that takes us within, for all spiritual practices lead us back to ourselves and prompt us to look within, with the light that is innate in our own beings!

At one of the most trying periods of my life, I was considering changing my religion to get around a dangerous problem I was faced with. I tried to reach out to my guru for guidance. At a time when I needed him the most, he made himself unavailable. When I was at the end of my tether, I had a dream. The guru handed me an old book and asked me to open it to any page. When I opened the book, the page I saw had written on it these words: 'Find all answers in your own self.' So, when I listened to my own inner voice attentively, I discovered there was a deep revulsion within me for the conversion I was considering. I also realized that instead of looking for the solution in myself, I was trying to look at conversion to solve the problem.

After attaining a sufficient degree of introversion with any spiritual tool or practice, we begin to gain insights into the innumerable ways in which the mind tricks us into habitual thought patterns. The same fears, expectations and aspirations keep on invading us. They are like arrows or bullets that are being aimed at us constantly.

The advantage of a mantra, for instance, is that we can jump across the mind without trying to understand it. But the mantra too will disappear one day after having purged the mind of all distractions. At this point, we will meet an obstacle that can be compared to a bucket hitting the muddy bottom of a well.

The trajectory of bhakti sadhana follows the same pattern. The deity first becomes closer to us than any person or any object including our own breath, and then suddenly vanishes. When we start praying intensely, we realize with a shock that there is nobody listening to us; that all prayers are a monologue. Now is the time to face the intractable problem looming large.

This is the moment when we encounter within ourselves an utter and terrifying emptiness, and it is this emptiness that we have been trying to avoid all this time, the reason that we have always been running towards things, throwing ourselves into endless pursuits and activities. This state of being has different names in different traditions. In Christian Mysticism, it is called the Dark Night of the Soul. In bhakti traditions, it is often compared to the most harrowing separation from the Beloved.

In experiential terms, the encounter with emptiness may also be the result of one's experiences of profound loss, and does not have to be an event only on the spiritual path. It could be the inability to cope with the death of a loved one or the estrangement from a beloved, which we refuse to accept. It could be the prospect of the loss of something we consider precious, be it wealth, name, fame, comfort or security. It could also be the feeling of being rejected. Whatever specific form the loss/emptiness takes, it is fundamentally the terror of loneliness or hopelessness. Any one of these experiences could be the dark room where we have left our keys, the trigger that can take us to the state of anuttara.

But this does not mean that grief or loss by itself can take a person there. It is how an individual responds to that state of darkness that makes the difference. In a rare individual, the state of total darkness and terror within can result in a total surrender of the self to the Divine.

Though this state is hard to describe in words, some great saint poets have given us a taste of it. Akka Mahadevi has this to say:

I was roasted in the heat caused by no fire, O mother
I pined in a wound caused by no bite, O mother
I became despondent without any happinesss, O mother
Because I loved Channamallikarjuna
I passed through worlds I should not have, O mother.

The seventeenth-century bhakti poet, Tukaram, likens this state to a kind of death:

The great ghost of Pandhari
Pounces upon everyone who passes by
That forest is haunted by many spirits.
Whoever enters it finds it maddening
O do not ever go there, you!

Nobody who goes in ever comes back
Only once did Tuka go to Pandhari
He hasn't been born ever since.[1]

How long does this state last and where does the rescue come from? This state of excruciating anguish may last a few months or years or a whole lifetime. This is the point at which most seekers give up and lapse back into the conditioned state. Only the most daring stick it out till the end. Atheistic schools like Buddhism ascribe the end of this agony to kammavipaka, the ripening of karmas. In theistic schools, it is attributed to the grace of the guru or the deity. These are words we use to describe the structural transformation within, according to our beliefs and backgrounds. Allama Prabhu calls it 'nijadudayada bedagina keela', 'the secret of the dawn of the true self'. Those following the path of devotional love compare the change to the reunion with the lost beloved. Some, like Kabir, resort to the language of paradox:

Everybody understands
The single drop merging into the ocean
One in a million comprehends
The ocean merging in a single drop.

---

[1] Subramaniam, Arundhathi (ed.). *Eating God: A Book of Bhakti Poetry.* Penguin Ananda, 2014.

The only way out with this emptiness is to accept it and embrace it; it is then that inner light dawns. What happens then is purely subjective and not easy to translate into words. The person who experiences anuttara realizes that he is not just an actor in the cosmic drama but he is also the playwright, the stage, the actor and the audience. He is all and all is him.

Anuttara is a permanent state. Many schools, particularly ascetic ones, consider this to be the end of the journey. But people can choose to return to the world of the senses in order to help mankind. Ramana Maharshi stayed in the state of anuttara for years. Sri Ramakrishna entered this state frequently and inhabited it for hours or days while living in the world. The Buddha chose not to dwell in blissful samadhi forever, and came back to the world to help awaken humanity. He returned because he saw sentient beings suffering and felt a deep compassion for all beings. It was then that he took an oath that he would not enter nibbana till the last blade of grass was released from suffering. However, because he had tasted nibbana, he could now function in the world without the limitations of a conditioned being.

For somebody enlightened, samsara and nibbana are the same. Mahayana Buddhist schools therefore consider mahakaruna, great compassion, to be of higher virtue than the attainment of nibbana. From this perspective, the dualism between the world and liberation breaks down. All is always part of the eternal Buddha-mind. One who lives in this state of fullness is free not only from the bondage of samsara but also from the bliss of nibbana. This state of unalloyed freedom, characterized by the Buddha's archetype, is called anuttara in Kashmir Shaivism and Mahayana Buddhism.

The fundamental insight of the ascended masters of Shaivism is that all is Shiva and Shiva is all. Their monistic view, like that of Mahayana, is uncompromising about the inherent unity of bondage and liberation. All is one; it is only the conditioned being that does not have the awareness that he is part of the One. Conditioned beings also partake of Shivahood without being aware of it. They have, at a deep level, chosen to give way to maya, the principle of obscuration and contraction. This is often compared to the condition of an actor who has chosen to play a role in a drama, identifying himself with the role and forgetting that his true self is independent of the joys and sorrows of his role. When knowledge of the identity of the self and Shiva dawns on the yogi, no matter which door he enters the practice through, or which method he employs, he is freed from the conditioned self.

The heightened states of samadhi in which yogis feel freed from suffering and other human limitations can be useful on the journey to our true home, anuttara. But if we become addicted to that state, it can become a trap. Yogis who are stuck at this point are called pralayakalas, half-yogis, who have burnt only their gross ignorance but have not yet destroyed the subtle ignorance, which is the limiting perception of dualism.

How Paramashiva, Universal Consciousness, who is none other than us, becomes entangled in the self-willed cosmic play, is described in a vak by Lalleshwari:

He came of Himself with Himself
And became engrossed in His own reflection
He Himself endeared his own Self
The Lord of Gauri hid Himself.

Allama Prabhu also describes the next part of the play – how he frees himself:

Look!
How I discovered that I am the fool
Who fell into maya's trap
Look!
How I discovered that I am Linga
Look!
How I discovered that I am Goggeshwara
Beyond sorrow and limitations
Putting up a play.

Here is a verse from a poem by Abhinavagupta on anuttara:

Whether it is real or unreal, huge or small, eternal or evanescent, all is sullied by maya, which is the same as the soul which, reflected in the mirror of pure consciousness and arising from your own self-awareness, unites with your essence. Realize and become established in this and celebrate the splendour of lordship of the cosmos.

As you will have understood by now, of all the doors and chambers introduced in this book, anuttara is the most difficult one to talk about. There is no set of demonstrable exercises or techniques that can take us there. It is a purely subjective state of unadulterated joy, tranquillity and fulfilment that can arise spontaneously, through the grace of a true guru or Universal Consciousness. It can be compared to the number 'zero' in the number system, which seems to have no value by itself but can enhance the numerical value of other numbers. Just as the number system is incomplete without zero, all the experiences of the other chambers described will be incomplete without anuttara, the ground and goal of all spiritual paths.

Yogis can attain immense spiritual power through sadhana associated with the different chambers/

spiritual techniques. However, such states of spiritual accomplishment are not irreversible. People may – and do – often fall into the trap of the limited mind when they begin to take advantage of their powers for selfish reasons. Anuttara, however, is an irreversible state. The deep and qualitative transformation it brings about can be compared to the transformation of base metal into gold in the process of alchemy. The gold subjected to alchemy cannot be turned into base metal again.

Another way of understanding anuttara is in the light of the concepts of the Shivagamas of Kashmir. According to their system, practitioners who are at different levels of evolution can be broadly classified into three categories:

- Those who exist in dvaita, the dualistic state, because they perceive the self and the world, the means and the end, as separate. They consider themselves a tiny atom in the vast cosmos, rather than one with the cosmos. The spiritual practices prescribed for them are called anavopaya, which include external rituals like going to temples, pilgrimages and doing physical asanas.
- Those who exist in dvaita-advaita, the dualistic-monistic state. Though they sometimes experience the oneness of everything, such people keep lapsing into the dualistic mindset. They need to do

more internal practices called pranopaya, which include pranayama, meditation and swara yoga/ kriya yoga. These methods are predominantly related to breath and mind.

• The third type of practitioner is already established in advaita, monistic state, and it is shambhavopaya that is suitable for such people. Those at this stage receive shaktipat directly from a guru or Paramashiva. The practices that need to be done at this stage start happening spontaneously without any conscious effort.

The highest of beings dwell in purnadvait, a completely monistic state. What they need is anupaya, no-practice, as their self has already blossomed into Shivahood, Buddha-mind or Ultimate Consciousness. Theirs is the state of anuttara, the unsurpassed state beyond which there is no other state to be attained. Here, speech and silence, sleep and wakefulness, action and inaction, become experiences and expressions of anuttara.

This classification is necessary for understanding anuttara intellectually to the extent possible. However, in actuality, from the perspective of anuttara, there is no linearity or hierarchy.

Kabir expresses anuttara cryptically in a simple but profound couplet thus:

Jal me kumbh, kumbh me jal, bahar bheetar pani
Toote kumbh jal jal hi samana ihthath kathyo gyani.

There is a pot in the water and water in the pot
There is water inside and outside
When the pot breaks water is still water
This is what the wise say.

Reading List

If you feel encouraged to explore your spiritual life after reading this book, here is a brief list for you. These are some of the books I have found very useful during my journey. I'd like you to remember that a book is not a substitute for the Guru, but there *are* books that can open a spiritual door for you in the absence of a guru.

First-hand accounts of authentic spiritual experiences can be very inspiring. *Kundalini: The Evolutionary Energy in Man* by Gopi Krishna is a remarkable book. So are the three volumes of *Aghora: At the Left Hand of God* by Robert Svoboda, which are based on the experiences and teachings of a great modern yogi called Vimalananda. You may also find some useful information in my book *Everyday Yogi*.

Books consisting of conversations with great saints are treasure troves of spiritual wisdom and of great practical value. *The Gospel of Ramakrishna* by Mahendranath Gupta is a great masterpiece in this genre. So are books by Nisargadatta Maharaj, particularly *I am That: Talks with Sri Nisargadatta Maharaj*. Ram Dass's *Miracle of Love: Stories about Neem Karoli Baba* is invaluable.

For books on body, breath and mind practice, I would recommend *Asana Pranayama Mudra Bandha* and *Meditations from the Tantras* by Swami Satyananda Saraswati. For those interested in the bhakti traditions, *Eating God: A Book of Bhakti Poetry* edited by Arundhathi Subramaniam is a good place to start.

Acknowledgements

If Poulomi Chatterjee, my publisher, had not suggested it, I would never have thought of writing a book like this. Thank you, Poulomi.

Who could have edited this book with greater care and sensitivity than Rukmini Chawla Kumar? Having worked with me on my previous book *Everyday Yogi*, she knows best when my writing works and when it falters. She never gives up till she gets me to say exactly what I want to convey. Thank you, Rukmini, for nursing this book. I would also like to thank Ansila Thomas for her careful proofreading.

My students Rojio, Astha, Priyanka and Dipanjali helped from time to time with the typing of the manuscript. I must thank them profusely.

My guru bhai, Prof Sreenivas Murthy, is a treasure-trove of information and wisdom in the realm of spirituality. His encouragement while writing this book was of great value.

My wife, Sandra, gave impetus by reading chapter after chapter and offering her comments for its improvement. This book owes a lot to her.

My former student Devapriya was the one who initiated this project by introducing me to Poulomi. How can I not thank her, though she disappeared thereafter.